Contents

Economic Development

6th Edition

Peter Cramp

informe

Thanks

Special thanks are due to my father, Dr A.B. Cramp, for reviewing the first draft of the first edition of this book and making numerous helpful suggestions.

My grateful thanks also to Professor David Elliott of the Energy Research Unit at the Open University, for pointing out an error in the previous edition.

To Annie, Joseph, Harry and Lucy

Using this book

This book includes a number of shaded boxes. The yellow shaded boxes (□) contain case studies or features on areas of interest related to the text. The green shaded boxes (□) are themed boxes covering a number of different constraints on development.

Anforme Ltd, Stocksfield Hall, Stocksfield, Northumberland NE43 7TN.

Typeset by George Wishart & Associates, Whitley Bay.
Printed by Potts Print (UK) Ltd.

An introduction to economic development

Unit 1: Introducing development and the Millennium Development Goals

Development and poverty

Levels of economic prosperity differ widely across the world, both within nations and between nations. In economies which we consider to be 'developed', the vast majority of people have access to the resources required to satisfy basic human material needs. In other words, few live in *absolute poverty*. However, wide variations in the distributions of income and wealth might lead us to conclude that many people in such countries live in *relative poverty*. Absolute poverty is a problem which affects large sections of the earth's population. Using a poverty line of $1.25 a day, Figure 1.1 suggests absolute poverty to be falling globally. A major reason for this is the growth and development of the Chinese economy.

Figure 1.1: Number of people in developing countries above and below $1.25 poverty line (billions)

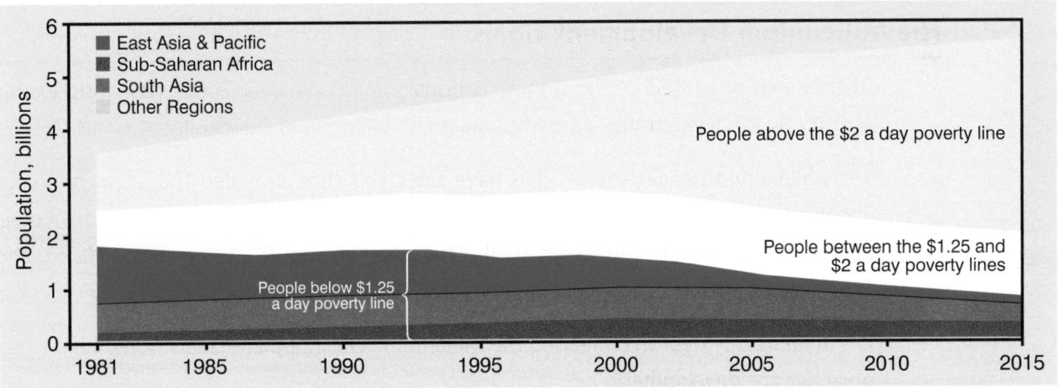

Source: World Bank

The study of the causes of absolute poverty, and potential solutions to this problem, is central to development economics. More generally, the subject is concerned with raising living standards. The economist Michael Todaro has identified three objectives of development:

1. To increase the availability and widen the distribution of basic life-sustaining goods

Former World Bank President Robert McNamara described absolute poverty as 'a condition of life so degraded by disease, illiteracy, malnutrition, and squalor as to deny its victims basic human necessities... life at the very margin of physical existence'. In doing so, he draws on the fact that human beings have a number of basic physical needs. Without food, drink, warmth, shelter, clothing and good health, life is threatened. Consequently, widespread provision of goods such as basic foodstuffs, clean water, housing, clothing and health care should perhaps be the primary objective of development. To this list we might add less obvious goods and services such as education, because survival can be threatened by lack of understanding of basic needs. Todaro's second and third objectives deal with enhancing the quality of life; guaranteeing continued survival is clearly a pre-condition for this to be possible.

2. To raise levels of living

Development strategies also seek to expand consumption possibilities beyond the level needed to guarantee survival. In other words, they attempt to raise income levels above the poverty line so that (i) More consumption is possible; (ii) Better quality goods and services become available. For example, clean water supplied to individual residences rather than a central pump for the community; (iii) A wider range of goods and services are accessible. These might include luxuries such as consumer durables (electrical goods, for example) and services such as entertainment.

Rising levels of income are not the only aspect of improved living standards. Todaro stresses that non-material factors are also important. Among these factors he identifies self-esteem, a person's sense of his own worth as a human being. Self-esteem is likely to be promoted by policies that widen the provision of basic necessities because such policies reflect a belief in the value of human life. However, policies which seek to impose the values and cultures of the developed world might cause anxiety and lack of self-esteem in developing countries. This is because an individual's self-esteem is likely to be rooted in the values of his own culture. It would therefore be questionable whether progress had been made if incomes rose at the expense of the destruction of shared values which hold a community together and give individuals a sense of belonging.

3. To expand the range of economic and social choices

This objective links in closely with the previous one. Without freedom to choose, living standards are likely to be low. A further concern of development is thus creating the conditions under which societies are free to choose their own economic and cultural direction. It is also about economic freedoms at the individual level including choices about the goods and services one consumes and the place in which one works. Individual political rights such as freedom of speech and worship are also important.

The Millennium Development Goals

At a summit organised by the United Nations (UN) in the year 2000, 189 world leaders promised to end poverty by 2015 when they agreed to meet the Millennium Development Goals (MDGs).

The Millennium Development Goals have since this time provided the major focus for efforts to reduce absolute poverty and are supported by the key international institutions involved in encouraging development, namely the World Bank, the International Monetary Fund (IMF), the Organisation for Economic Cooperation and Development (OECD) and the UN itself.

It is immediately clear that meeting the Millennium Development Goals would help to satisfy Todaro's three objectives of development.

One of the Millenium Development Goals is to eradicate poverty and hunger.

The Millennium Development Goals

1. **Eradicate poverty and hunger.** Halve, between 1990 and 2015, the proportion of people whose income is less than $1.25 a day.

2. **Achieve universal primary education.** Ensure that, by 2015, children everywhere, boys and girls alike, will be able to complete a course of primary schooling.

3. **Promote gender equality and empower women.** Eliminate gender disparity in primary and secondary education, preferably by 2005, and in all levels of education no later than 2015.

4. **Reduce child mortality.** Reduce by two-thirds, between 1990 and 2015, the under 5 mortality rate.

5. **Improve maternal health.** Reduce by three-quarters, between 1990 and 2015, the maternal mortality ratio.

6. **Combat HIV/AIDS, malaria and other diseases.** Have halted by 2015, and begun to reverse, the spread of HIV/AIDS and incidence of malaria and other diseases.

7. **Ensure environmental sustainability.** Halve, by 2015, the proportion of people without sustainable access to safe drinking water.

8. **Build a global partnership for development.** All international economies work toward achieving the Millennium Development Goals through increased development assistance, debt reduction, reduced barriers to trade, and special efforts to address the needs of poorest countries.

Progress towards the Millennium Development Goals

The focus provided by the MDGs has helped to bring about some remarkable achievements over the past few years. Examples of these achievements include:

- The poverty reduction target was reached five years ahead of schedule in 2010. In developing regions, the proportion of people living on less than $1.25 a day fell from 47% in 1990 to 22% in 2010. However, 1.2 billion people in the world still live in extreme poverty.

- Between 1990 and 2010, mortality rates from malaria fell by more than 25% globally and death rates from tuberculosis are on target to be halved by 2015.

- Since 1990, more than 2.1 billion people have gained access to safe drinking water.

Despite these successes, the UN Millennium Development Goals Report of 2013 suggested that a number of goals were unlikely to be met by 2015.

- Environmental sustainability is under severe threat with the growth in global carbon dioxide emissions accelerating and today's carbon dioxide emissions more than 46% above their 1990 level.

- Maternal deaths in child-birth fell by 47% in the two decades to 2010, but it was looking unlikely that the target of a 75% reduction would be met.

- The goal of promoting gender equality has proven particularly difficult to meet.

Figure 1.2 shows progress towards the Millennium Development Goals and highlights that some goals have already been achieved or surpassed, while for others, such as the Primary completion rate serious shortfalls still persist.

Figure 1.2: Progress towards the Millennium Development Goals

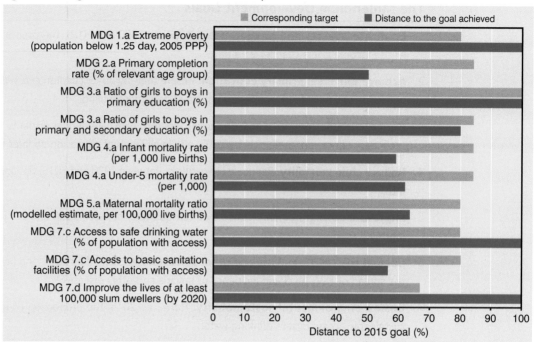

Source: World Bank, Global Monitoring Report 2013

What happens after 2015?

It is likely that on 1st January 2016 the Millennium Development Goals (MDGs) will be replaced by new objectives known as the Sustainable Development Goals (SDGs), with the aim of building on the progress already made. It can be argued that while the MDGs have not fully been accomplished, much more has been achieved than would have been the case without them and that governments around the world have been spurred into action by their existence. The goals were focused on a simple message of tackling poverty and backed by as many as 189 countries.

If the new SDGs are to be successful, similar focus and backing are likely to be needed. This may prove difficult to achieve. Widespread consultation is taking place about what the SDGs should be and the range of possible objectives under discussion is vast.

Writing in *The Guardian*, Stanislav Saling (a communications adviser at the UN Development Programme) notes that "the scope of discussed post-2015 SDGs is so expansive that it stretches from the anti-poverty MDGs to new territories like improving road safety, ending tax havens and preserving indigenous cultures." He continues by observing that "purely from a communications perspective, SDGs cannot be all things to all people. More issues mean less clarity; less clarity means decreased impact."

The *Girl Effect* is one example of an attempt to influence the new post-2015 agenda. This organisation states that "Girls were left out of the MDGs and the *Girl Declaration* has been written to make sure it doesn't happen again." The *Girl Declaration* was created after consulting 508 adolescent girls in 14 countries about what they needed to have a chance to reach their potential and it recommends five goals for sustainable development written around the needs of girls, and the accompanying indicators by which they might be monitored. In the words of the group, "every sustainable development solution begins with girls."

While the *Girl Effect* may succeed in influencing the post 2015 agenda to some degree, the *Girl Declaration* is unlikely to be adopted in its entirety. With many other groups competing for influence it may prove a challenge to bring the same clarity and focus to the SDGs as was enjoyed by the MDGs, but doing it is a key factor in continuing to achieve development progress.

Classification of development

A number of different terms are used in classifying the economies of the world. Perhaps the simplest system of classification is to divide the world into three categories. A small group of rich, industrialised countries are known as *developed* or *First World countries*. These are contrasted with a large group of poorer countries known as *developing* or *Third World countries*.

Figure 2.1: The classification of development

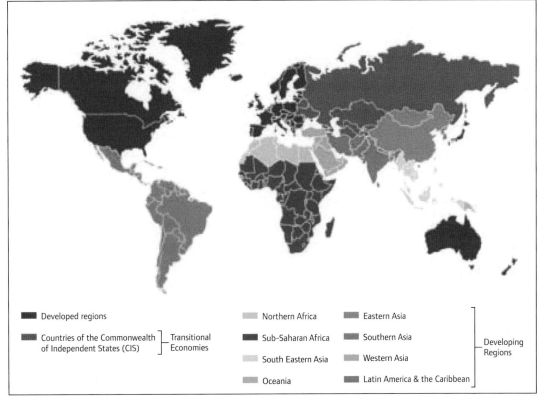

Source: United Nations Millennium Development Goals Report 2010

The other category consists of former economies of the Soviet Union (USSR), which have grouped together to form the Commonwealth of Independent States (CIS). They are known as *transitional economies* because they are in the process of changing from a planned to a free-market economic system. They are occasionally termed *Second World* countries, although the use of first-second-third world terminology is generally in decline.

From a geographical perspective, most developed countries lie in the western side of the northern hemisphere. The exceptions to this rule are Australia, New Zealand and Japan. The vast majority of the southern hemisphere countries are developing nations. It is clear, therefore, that something of a divide exists between northern and southern countries of the world.

The economies comprising the developed world are broadly similar to one another. Stark contrasts, on the other hand, exist amongst developing nations. For this reason, Third World countries are often divided into *low income* and *middle income* countries. Some of the middle income countries are termed *emerging economies* because of their fast growth. If they have already developed a western style economy they are known as *newly industrialised countries*. A number of East Asian economies fall into this category. Following industrialisation, countries such as Singapore, Malaysia, Hong Kong and South Korea have achieved rapid economic growth.

In summary, classification is as follows:

	Developed countries	Transitional economies	Developing countries
Alternative terminology	First world; Western economies	Second world; Commonwealth of Independent States (CIS)	Third world; Less developed countries (LDCs)
Geographical location	West of northern hemisphere; East Asia (Japan); extreme south east (Australia and New Zealand)	Eastern Europe and Asia	Southern hemisphere
Sub-categories	G7 countries (USA, Canada, France, Italy, Germany, UK, Japan) or G8 with the inclusion of Russia	Former USSR countries	Low income countries; Middle income countries; Emerging economies; Newly industrialised countries (NICs)

Measurement of development

National income/national output

The most common method for measuring development, and one of the simplest, is to use figures for national income or national output. The two are equal to each other by definition, as the concept of the *circular flow of income* demonstrates. Each measures the same flow of economic activity but at a different stage.

Various measures of national income are used for purposes of comparison, but the two most popular are *gross domestic product* (GDP) and *gross national product* (GNP). GDP measures all the income generated within the economy in question, regardless of who it accrues to. In practice, some of the income generated within any economy will belong to residents of other countries, because they own the factors of production which have generated that income. The reverse is also true; there will be some inflow of income too, because some domestic residents will own factors of production which have been used to generate income in other countries. By making the relevant adjustments to GDP to account for this, we obtain GNP, defined as all the income accruing to residents of a particular country regardless of where that income was generated. If we are concerned with living standards within a given nation, we will be more concerned with the income of its citizens than with how much income was generated within the domestic economy. GNP is therefore the better indicator for this purpose.

GNP = GDP + income generated abroad but accruing to domestic residents – income generated in the domestic economy but accruing to foreign residents.

However, simply to use GNP as a measure of the economic well-being of a country's residents, and hence as a proxy statistic for the level of development, would be very misleading. Obtaining a definitive measure of development is impossible, but there are a number of adjustments that can be made to GNP to gain a more appropriate indicator:

1. **Conversion to per capita figures.** Any given level of GNP represents a much higher standard of living for a nation with a small population than for a nation with a large one. It is possible to adjust for this by measuring income per capita (per person). GNP per capita is obtained by dividing a country's raw GNP figure by its population.

2. **Adjusting for unrecorded economic activity.** In most developing nations, much activity takes place on a *subsistence basis*. Families produce as much as they can to support themselves but have little left

over to trade. Untraded activity cannot be recorded. Equally, trade in the *black-market* (the 'informal economy') is not recorded in national income statistics.

3. **Taking account of income distribution.** A concern for a nation's living standards would seem to imply a concern for the well-being of all its citizens. In Unit 1 it was observed that often the benefits of economic growth are concentrated in the hands of relatively few people; national income can be very unequally distributed. Accordingly, a high per capita GNP figure could give a misleading picture of general living standards within a country. An economist would want to supplement per capita GNP data with information on how equally, or otherwise, income is distributed (see the section on income distribution later in this unit).

4. **The need to use real data when comparing per capita GNP over time.** For most countries a comparison of per capita GNP now with, say, 50 years ago, would make little sense if the raw data was used. This is because prices are not at the same levels as 50 years ago. The question arises, of a given increase in per capita GNP how much is taken up by price increases? Only if the per capita GNP has risen by more than prices will the material well-being, that is the quantity of goods and services that the average citizen can buy, have increased. To conduct a valid comparison between now and fifty years ago, we must either adjust today's figure downwards by the extent of inflation in the intervening period or adjust the figure from fifty years ago upwards. The raw figures are called *nominal data* and the adjusted figures *real data*.

5. **The need to convert to a common currency when comparing between countries.** The choice of the exchange rates to use for conversion is crucial. It is desirable to use the *purchasing power parity* (PPP) rate. This is the rate which would allow a traveller between the countries in question to convert his money between the relevant currencies and be able to purchase the same quantity of goods and services regardless of which country he was in. The use of PPP rates is important because they account for the fact that a dollar typically buys more goods in a developing country than a developed one.

6. **Adjustments to take account of a variety of other factors.** A number of other difficulties call into question the accuracy of the per capita GNP figure as an indicator of living standards. These include *accounting errors*. Even in nations with sophisticated accounting procedures, GNP data is subject to revision for some years after it is initially published. This is due to the uncovering of errors. The scope for errors is likely to be even greater in developing countries with more rudimentary accounting methods. We would also wish to take into account the *geographical area* of a country. The broader the area that a country's population inhabits, the more of GNP that will be taken up by the cost of transportation of goods from one area to another. Other things being equal, if two countries have the same per capita GNP the country with the smaller geographical area is likely to have higher living standards. Similar observations can be made with regard to *differences in climate* between countries. A country with a cold climate will have to spend more of its GNP on heating and insulation than a country with a warmer climate. Again, of two countries with the same per capita GNP it is likely that the country with the warmer climate will have the higher living standards.

The distribution of income

Many modern development economists are as much concerned with the distribution of income as with its level. Because of this, it is useful to have a quantifiable measure of the extent of inequality within a nation.

A first step towards such a measure is a graphical device known as a *Lorenz curve*. A Lorenz curve plots the percentage of a nation's income which is enjoyed by the poorest 'x' per cent of the nation's population. The curve is drawn for values of 'x' between 0 and 100. It might be the case, for example, that the poorest 10% of a nation's population enjoy only 1% of its income. Accordingly we would plot 10 on the horizontal axis against 1 on the vertical axis. If the poorest 15% of the population enjoy 1.7% of income, we would plot a point relating to these figures. Note that the poorest 15% of the population include the poorest

10%: the further we go to the right on the horizontal axis, the more of the population is included. We therefore label the horizontal axis as 'cumulative percentage of the population'. By similar reasoning, the vertical axis is ' cumulative percentage of income'.

Two hypothetical Lorenz curves are shown in Figure 2.2. In each case, the diagonal line represents complete equality in the distribution of income: the poorest 10% of the population receive 10% of income, the poorest 50% of the population enjoy 50% of the income and so on. The further the Lorenz curve bows away from the diagonal, the greater the degree of inequality which is depicted. Below, the nation represented in Figure 2.2(b) has a higher degree of inequality than the nation shown in 2.2(a).

Figure 2.2: Lorenz curves

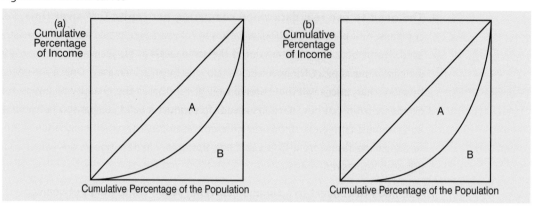

It is now possible to derive a numerical measure of inequality, known as the *Gini coefficient*. The area under the diagonal in both graphs shown in Figure 2.2 has been divided by the Lorenz curve into two sections, A and B. The Gini coefficient is defined as the area between the diagonal and the Lorenz curve divided by the total area under the diagonal or, in terms of Figure 2.2:

$$\text{Gini coefficient} = \frac{\text{Section A}}{\text{Section A} + \text{Section B}}$$

A Gini coefficient of zero indicates complete equality, while a Gini coefficient of one represents total inequality (one person enjoying all of the nation's income!). In general, the higher the Gini coefficient, the greater the degree of inequality. This is borne out by again inspecting Figure 2.2. Because the area under the diagonal is the same in both parts (a) and (b), but section A is greater in part (b) than part (a), it follows that the Gini coefficient is greater in Figure 2.2(b) than Figure 2.2(a).

It is, of course, possible to quote the Gini coefficient as a percentage figure. For instance, a Gini coefficient of 0.43 is the same as one of 43%.

Data on Gini coefficients for some developing nations can be found in Unit 3, in Table 3.1 (Income, its distribution and prevalence of poverty).

Other indicators

A host of other statistics can be useful in gauging the extent of a country's economic development. Access to basic services is important. The percentage of population receiving safe water supplies might be taken as particularly significant, and the percentage of the population with adequate shelter. Access to other services such as electricity should also be taken into account. We might wish to consider data on health, including the availability of medical care (e.g. the population divided by the number of doctors), rates of malnutrition and mortality rates. The quality of education could be examined using literacy rates and data on levels of qualifications.

Labour statistics are also helpful. The less developed a country is, the more of its population tend to work in agriculture, for example, with fewer in industry. Measurements of labour productivity (output per worker) are also significant; under-developed countries tend to be characterised by low labour productivity.

The percentage of population having safe water supplies is an important development indicator.

The UN's Human Development Index (HDI)

The Human Development Index (HDI) is a summary index that measures three basic aspects of human development, namely:

- longevity
- knowledge
- a decent standard of living.

For the purposes of calculating the HDI, standard of living is measured by GDP per capita (converted into US$ at purchasing power parity exchange rates). This recognises that, all other things being equal, economic growth increases development. However, the inclusion of longevity and knowledge recognises that there are other aspects of development. In the HDI, longevity is measured by life expectancy at birth. Knowledge is measured by a combination of the adult literacy rate and the combined primary, secondary, and tertiary education gross enrolment ratio.

The HDI is better at capturing levels of development than per capita GDP figures alone. However, it remains incomplete. This is true of any single development indicator. No single figure can capture all the different aspects of development and their complexity. Examples of facets of development not covered by the HDI include levels of political participation and gender inequalities.

It is an interesting exercise to compare per capita GDP figures with the HDI. Some countries fare much better in the HDI rankings than they do in the per capita income table. A good example is Cuba, which, based on the 2013 Human Development Report, came 44 places higher in the HDI rankings than its position for GDP. Communist Cuba remains a planned economy and does little trade, helping to explain its relatively low income per capita, but it does place strong emphasis on other factors, such as education, which support its HDI performance. On the other hand, the United Arab Emirates came 31 places lower in the HDI rankings than in the per capita GDP table. Such discrepancies are common in oil-rich nations. Oil revenues boost per capita income, but the benefits tend to be concentrated in the hand of relatively few people. Thus the oil revenue is of little use in the wider context of development. Table 2.1 gives HDI data for selected countries.

An immediate understanding of how two countries with similar per capita income can score very differently in HDI terms can be gained by looking at Figure 2.3. Life expectancy and adult literacy rates are much higher in Nepal than in Afghanistan, despite their similar incomes.

Table 2.1: Human Development Index, selected countries

	HDI value 2012	HDI rank 2012	Per capita Gross National Income (GDI) rank 2012
Top 5 ranking countries			
Norway	0.955	1	5
Australia	0.938	2	16
USA	0.937	3	7
Netherlands	0.921	4	9
Germany	0.920	5	11
Bottom 5 ranking countries			
Burkina Faso	0.343	183	170
Chad	0.340	184	164
Mozambique	0.327	185	176
DR Congo	0.304	186	186
Niger	0.304	186	182
Other selected countries			
UK	0.875	26	21
China	0.699	101	90
India	0.554	136	133

Source: United Nations Human Development Report 2013

Figure 2.3: Similar income, different human development

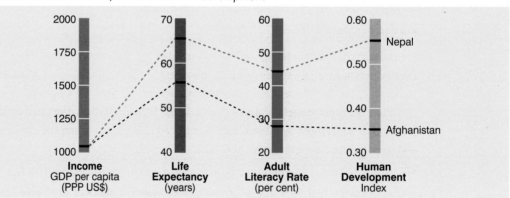

Source: Adapted from UN Human Development Report

Meanwhile, Figure 2.4 offers a visual impression of HDI performance by region. The data suggests continuous improvements in human development across all regions.

Figure 2.4: Regional HDI scores

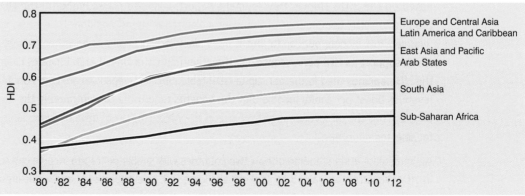

Source: United Nations Development Programme

The Human Poverty Index (HPI-1 and HPI-2)

While the HDI measures overall progress in achieving economic development, the human poverty index (HPI) reflects the distribution of that progress and resulting deprivation. Where progress is distributed very unequally, it is likely that poverty will exist. Poverty can be measured as a lack of income, but, in practice, poverty includes other deprivations too, such as lack of choices and opportunities.

The HPI draws upon data for longevity, knowledge and living standards, much as the HDI does. The difference is that it focuses on deprivation. So, while in the HDI longevity is measured by life expectancy at birth, in the HPI it is measured by the probability of **not** surviving to a certain age. While the HDI concentrates on **adult literacy rates** and enrolment ratios for education, the HPI focuses on **adult illiteracy**.

The HPI is split into two different indicators. HPI-1 is used for developing nations, HPI-2 for developed countries. There are small differences in the indicators used. For example, HPI-1 uses the probability at birth of not surviving until the age of **40**. HPI-2 for developed countries uses the age of 60 instead. HPI-2 also attempts to measure '**social exclusion**' which is not measured by the HDI or the HPI-1 index.

The make up of the HDI, HPI-1 and HPI-2 indices is shown in the box below:

Index	Longevity	Knowledge	Decent standard of living	Participation or exclusion
HDI	Life expectancy at birth	1. Adult literacy rate 2. Combined enrolment ratio	GDP per capita (PPP US$)	Not applicable
HPI-1 (developing countries)	Probability at birth of not surviving until age 40	Adult illiteracy rate	Deprivation measured by: 1. Percentage of people not using improved water sources 2. Percentage of children under 5 who are underweight	Not applicable
HPI-2 (developed countries)	Probability at birth of not surviving to age 60	Percentage of adults lacking functional literacy skills	Percentage of people living below the poverty line (50% of median disposable household income)	Long-term unemployment rate (12 months or more)

Source: UN Human Development Report

The Index of Sustainable Economic Welfare (ISEW)

The Index of Sustainable Economic Welfare (ISEW) is put forward as an alternative to measuring living standards and development using solely GDP. It places particular emphasis on the environmental sustainability of economic activity.

The following comment on the ISEW comes from Friends of the Earth: "This is an attempt to measure the part of economic activity that genuinely increases the quality of life. For example, it makes a subtraction for air pollution caused by economic activity, and makes an addition to count unpaid household labour – such as cleaning or child minding. It also covers areas such as income inequality, other environmental damage, and depletion of environmental assets."

The ISEW is a highly controversial indicator. For example, it has been criticised for introducing subjective measures of the value of environmental damage to produce what some people will misinterpret as an objective economic indicator.

Unit 3: Similarities and differences between developing countries

Similarities

The nations in developing regions are diverse in many ways. For this reason, it is difficult and dangerous for economists to prescribe a set of policies to be applied universally amongst developing nations. However it is both possible and helpful in structuring our thinking to identify some characteristics that developing nations share.

Similarities include:

1. **Low living standards.** There are a number of characteristics of low living standards. These include low per capita income combined with high income inequality; widespread absolute poverty; lack of access to resources required to meet basic needs; malnutrition, poor health and short life spans. Tables 3.1 and 3.2 offer data on some of these factors.

Table 3.1: Income, its distribution and the prevalence of poverty

Country	Gross National Income per capita ($), 2012*	Poverty (% of people living on under $1.25 a day)[†]	Gini Coefficient[†]
Tanzania	1590	67.9	37.6
Ethiopia	1140	39.0	29.8
Zambia	1620	68.5	51.0
Kenya	1760	43.4	47.7
Pakistan	3030	21.0	30.0
India	3840	32.7	33.4
Madagascar	950	81.3	44.1
Peru	10240	4.9	48.1
Dominican Rep	9820	2.2	47.2
Brazil	11270	6.1	54.7
Thailand	9430	<2	40.0
Poland	21170	<2	34.1
Italy	32870	–	36.0
Sweden	44150	–	25.0
United Kingdom	36880	–	36.0
China	9210	13.1	42.5

*Purchasing power parity estimates [†]Based on most recent available data; year varies from country to country
Source: Adapted from World Bank, World Development Report 2014 and United Nations, Human Development Report 2013

2. **Low productivity of factors of production.** For example, labour productivity tends to be low. This is largely because of shortages of complementary resources, including physical capital, and their poor quality where they are available. Physical capital includes machines and premises together with infrastructure investments such as roads, railways and utilities (telephones, electricity, water etc.). This imposes constraints on firms as shown in Figure 3.1. Also, lack of access to education means that levels of human capital are often low. However, Figure 3.2 indicates that some developing countries have made substantial progress in widening access to education. Some have even achieved near universal access to primary education. This reflects a belief in the importance of education as part of the development process and offers hope of improved labour productivity in the years to come.

3. **High population growth**, expected to average 2.3 per cent annually between 2010 and 2015 in the least developed countries. The average for developed countries is 0.33 per cent. A full discussion of population growth and associated problems can be found in Unit 13.

Table 3.2: Health indicators and life expectancy

Country	Health expenditure per capita (US$), 2011	Malnutrition (% of under 5) 2008-2012*	Life expectancy at birth (males), 2011
Mozambique	35	15.6	49
Ethiopia	17	29.2	58
Uganda	42	14.1	53
Jamaica	271	3.2	71
Romania	500	–	71
Poland	899	–	73
Brazil	1121	–	70
Chile	1075	0.5	76
Saudi Arabia	758	–	73
South Africa	689	–	52
Singapore	2286	–	80
Spain	3027	–	79
United Kingdom	3609	–	79
United States	8608	–	76

Source: Adapted from World Bank, World Development Report 2010 and 2014 and United Nations, Human Development Report 2009, WHO
*Based on most recent available data; year varies from country to country

Figure 3.1: More than half of firms in South Asia and Sub-Saharan Africa say that lack of reliable electricity is a major constraint to business

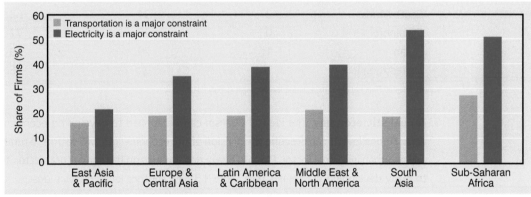

Source: World Bank, World Development Report 2010

Figure 3.2: Adjusted net enrolment rate in primary education (%)

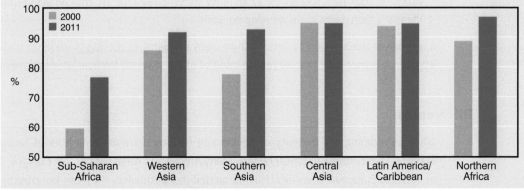

Source: UN Millennium Development Goals Report 2013

4. **High levels of unemployment** (resources, especially labour, that are not used) and underemployment (resources which are used for only part of the time, for example a worker who is only employed for part of the working week).

5. **A narrowly focused economy**, commonly with dependence on agriculture and export of primary products. Table 3.3 indicates that this remains particularly true of many African countries. In lots of other developing countries, the structure of the economy is now more diverse, but with agriculture still contributing a large proportion of GDP.

Table 3.3: Structure of production, % of GDP, 2008

Country	Agriculture	Industry	Services
Ethiopia	44	18	42
Mozambique	29	24	47
Tanzania	45	17	37
Uganda	23	26	52
India	17	29	54
China	11	49	53
Pakistan	20	27	53
Romania	7	25	68
Jamaica	5	25	69
Poland	5	21	65
Brazil	7	28	65
Mexico	4	37	59
Bangladesh	19	29	52
South Africa	3	34	63
Singapore	0	28	72
Japan	1	29	69
United Kingdom	1	24	76

Source: Adapted from the World Bank, World Development Report 2010

6. **A dualistic economy.** The idea of dualism can be applied to developing economies in a number of ways. At one level it can describe the division of the economy into two sectors, a rural agricultural sector and an urban industrial sector. Despite heavy dependence on the agricultural sector, this division applies to many developing economies (see Table 3.3). At another level, dualism describes division between groups of the population in terms of living standards and economic opportunities. This is characterised by unequal access to resources and high income inequality. Signs of such dualism are present in Tables 3.1 to 3.3. One group which tends to be particularly disadvantaged in developing economies is women. Economic indicators such as life expectancy confirm this to be so, with females typically having shorter life spans than males in the developing world.

It is apparent that developing nations share many problems. In seeking to understand development issues, however, it is important that we remain mindful of the many differences among developing countries.

Differences

When considering the diversity of developing nations there are a number of factors that we should examine. These include historical factors. Many African and Asian nations, for example, are former colonies of Western European countries. Having gained independence, they can be expected to devote some attention to re-moulding their economic and political institutions, possibly at the expense of rapid economic growth. In contrast, Latin America has a longer history of political independence.

A dualistic developing economy can refer to a rural agricultural sector and an urban industrial sector.

It should be recognised that the potential for development depends on the interaction between economics and politics. Some economic policies, for example, might be ruled out by the power of certain groups such as the military, bankers and foreign manufacturers. The lessons of history suggest that a stable political and legal system is essential in fostering growth. In recent decades, Asian countries with such stability have been able to make spectacular progress while the economies of more politically volatile countries have stagnated.

Amongst developing nations, as with the rest of the world, the current trend is for more private sector and less public sector activity. There remain, however, very substantial differences in the mix of economic activity between developing countries. As a general observation, it tends to be the case that Latin American and Southeast Asian nations have larger private sectors than South Asian and African nations.

A country's resource endowment, in both physical and human terms, is important in determining its growth potential. The land in some countries is much more fertile than others, while some are blessed with access to minerals or oil. The size of a nation has an important influence on its resource endowment. The larger a nation is territorially, the greater the stock of physical resources it is likely to have at its disposal. The larger a nation is in terms of population, the more workers it has available, and the more extensive the possible division of labour, although the quality of the workforce depends very much on the availability of good education. Despite these advantages, large size also creates problems. At the simplest level, a higher population means more people for a country's economy to support. Beyond this, there could be difficulties including tension between different sections of the population (on ethnic or religious grounds, perhaps) and regional economic imbalances.

Geographical factors are significant in determining the extent to which international trade can play an important role in development. A country which is in close proximity to nations in the developed world has a real advantage with regard to exporting to them, as transport costs will be much lower than for the exports of a more remote nation. Equally, a land-locked nation is at a disadvantage in the international trade arena relative to those with a coast-line. This is because the majority of the world's trade still takes place by sea (see Unit 4 for more details).

Conflict as a constraint on development

A feature held in common by many, but not all, less developed countries (LDCs) is vulnerability to armed conflicts. These are sometime conflicts with neighbouring countries and sometimes internal conflicts (civil wars) between different groups within the country. The existence of poverty may be a cause of such conflict, but the conflict itself acts to increase poverty and hinder development

The graph below details the number of people forced to move either internally within a country or as refugees to another country, with war being the predominant cause.

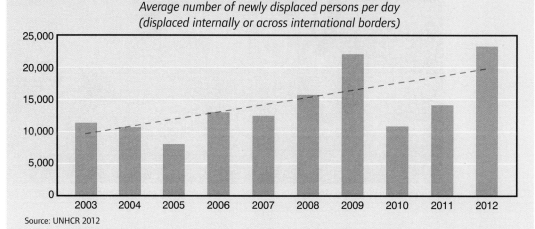

Average number of newly displaced persons per day
(displaced internally or across international borders)

Source: UNHCR 2012

It is not difficult to see ways in which armed conflict may damage development. These include:

- The destruction of physical capital during the course of the conflict.
- The diversion of labour resources from production to fighting.
- The death of valuable labour resources. Some of those killed may have high levels of human capital.
- The diversion of investment to expenditure on military capital rather than projects focused on poverty relief.
- Loss of economic confidence deterring investment.
- The loss of vital institutions during the course of conflict, especially financial institutions. Banks are likely to pull out of war torn countries, removing the channels through which funds are lent by savers to those who wish to borrow for investment purposes.

It is unsurprising that as a result of factors such as those listed above, conflict affected areas (which are shown below as countries in fragile situations) have made slow progress towards achieving the Millennium Development Goals:

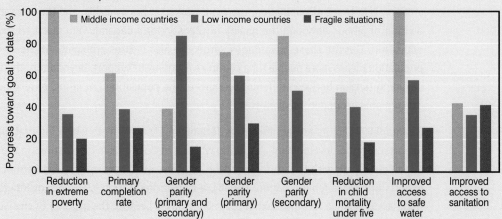

Source: World Development Report 2014

History: The causes and consequences of the current international division of labour

The global pattern of production and trade during the late 18th century and for the majority of the 19th century was influenced greatly by colonialism. Serving the interests of their masters (notably Britain, France, Holland and Spain, amongst other European nations) colonies were required to concentrate on primary sector activities. Agricultural products were grown and exported, and raw materials such as minerals extracted. Meanwhile, the profits derived from colonial possessions helped to further industrialisation amongst the 'mother countries'. Profits which were saved added to the supply of loanable funds available to the banking system. Consequently, interest rates were lowered making it more attractive to borrow for investment purposes.

While the division of labour described above was largely dictated by colonialism, it was reinforced by the natural working of markets. The increase in supply of manufactured products caused by the industrial revolution drove prices for these goods down. The *terms of trade*, therefore, moved in favour of those nations specialising in primary sector produce. In other words the price of primary sector produce was now higher relative to prices of manufactured goods. It appeared to many less developed countries that they could enjoy future growth by specialising in primary production. To their cost, this has proved not to be the case. Exporters of primary produce have suffered downturns in their terms of trade since 1880, caused, amongst other things, by increasing world supply in this sector.

Today's division of labour has implications for the future. A country's choice of areas in which to specialise should take into account not just current conditions, but also those likely to prevail in the future. To that end, successful development might require substantial state involvement in the economy, fostering those sectors which are likely to find lucrative export markets in future years. This is the experience shared both by developed countries and the newly industrialised countries of East Asia.

A colonial building in Goa, India. Colonialism was a major influence on the pattern of trade and production in the late 18th and 19th centuries.

A narrow economic structure as a constraint on development

As explained above, history has contributed to the narrow structure of many developing economies today. Narrow economic structures are particularly common in African economies. Single agricultural commodities can account for substantial proportions of a nation's exports and in turn of the nation's income. Cashew nuts comprise around 93% of the exports earnings of Guinea-Bissau, coffee 70% in Burundi and tobacco 54% in Malawi. Malawi derives around half of its national income from the sale of tobacco leaves.

Dependence on oil exports is also common. Angola earns 97% of all its export revenues from oil, for example, and a number of other African countries over 80% as shown below:

Oil revenue as a % of export earnings, selected African countries

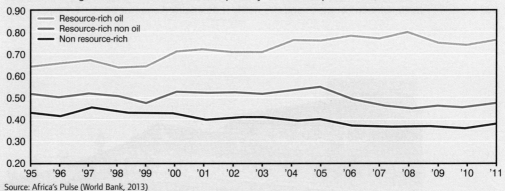

Source: African Competitiveness Report 2013, World Bank

The export concentration ratio measures the degree to which a country's exports are focused on a small number of products or small number of trading partners. A high export concentration ratio is common amongst resource rich countries, especially those who possess oil, as shown here:

Source: Africa's Pulse (World Bank, 2013)

Dependence on one product or even one sector of the economy, like agriculture, carries a number of problems. These include:

- Vulnerability to the effects of disease or weather on the crop.

- Exposure to long term price falls as global supply increases due to higher productivity.

- The danger of diminishing marginal returns as large quantities of labour are employed in a sector with limited land and capital equipment.

- The danger of soil degradation due to over-cultivation.

- Unfair competition due to subsidies given by developed nations to their own producers in these markets.

- The limited potential of agricultural commodities as a source of economic growth, suggesting that development will be difficult unless economic diversification occurs.

These factors are discussed in more detail later in the book.

Geography: Resource endowments and access to international markets

The natural resources of developing countries differ widely. Some developing countries are resource rich in the sense that they may have land containing precious minerals, metals or oil, or, alternatively, favourable climates. Also, areas of natural beauty are a substantial geographical advantage in encouraging tourism. *Ceteris paribus*, one would expect that resource rich countries would achieve stronger economic performance than countries with less favourable endowments, but this has not always been the case. The reasons for this are not clear, but one possible explanation is that riches of a particular resource may encourage a narrow economic structure and all the problems referred to in the previous section.

Due to the importance of trade in encouraging economic growth and development, those countries with access to the sea (for transport of goods) and in close proximity to the markets of developed countries (again reducing transport costs) have a natural advantage.

Geography as a constraint on development

"Many of the world's poorest countries are severely hindered by high transport costs because they are landlocked; situated in high mountain ranges; or lack navigable rivers, long coastlines, or good natural harbours. Culture does not explain the persistence of poverty in Bolivia, Ethiopia, Kyrgyzstan, or Tibet. Look instead to the mountain geography of a landlocked region suffering crushing transport costs and economic isolation that stifle nearly all forms of modern activity."

The End of Poverty, Jeffrey Sachs

United Nations data suggest that transport costs account for 14.1% of the value of exports from landlocked countries, 17.2% of the exports of the least developed countries but only 4.5% of exports from developed market economies. It is clear that geography has given a poor hand to many of the poorest countries in the world.

Other ways in which geography can hinder development include a dry climate that is not conducive to food production or a tropical climate that favours the spread of diseases such as malaria.

The obstacles presented by geography are probably not insurmountable, but they do imply that development will be more difficult and expensive to achieve. This is an expense that the poorest countries are unlikely to afford without outside help.

Development – theories and strategies

Unit 5: The economics of growth

Economic growth and development

It is generally accepted that economic growth in low income countries is *necessary* in order to achieve the objectives of development, such as the alleviation of absolute poverty.

However, it is also widely accepted that economic growth is not *sufficient* to guarantee that the objectives of development are met. The primary effects of poverty are felt by individuals but the level of a nation's income is an aggregate measure for the whole economy. It is entirely possible that the benefits of growth could be concentrated in the hands of relatively few people, perhaps those who were already enjoying good standards of living.

It is possible to argue that even if the benefits of growth are initially distributed unequally that all sections of society will eventually benefit through what is popularly known as the *'trickle-down effect'*. For example, the demand of the wealthy sections of society for a wide range of consumer goods and services may create employment opportunities for others.

However, empirical evidence has shown that strong economic growth can sometimes be accompanied by stubbornly high levels of poverty. Development strategies are more likely to be focused directly on alleviating poverty and less on stimulating economic growth than in the past. While growth is still desirable, it should be 'high quality growth' that brings lasting gains in employment and living standards and reduces poverty.

Growth of the global economy as a whole is considered important to help meet the objectives of development. High levels of global income help to support demand for exports of agricultural produce and manufactured goods from the developing world, for example. Falling global income in 2008 and early 2009, and slow growth in the following years, hindered the achievement of development objectives (see Figure 5.1) despite the fact that the GDP growth of emerging and developed economies continued to outperform advanced economies.

Figure 5.1: Global GDP growth, %, quarter-on-quarter, annualised

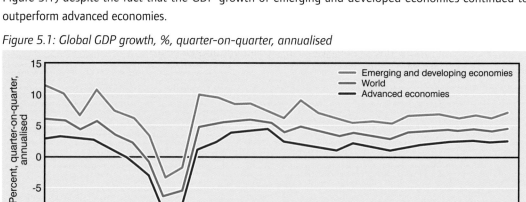

Source: IMF

Potential output

One definition of *economic growth* is that of an increase in the capacity, or potential output, of an economy. Potential output is the maximum that an economy can produce if it uses available factors of production efficiently. By expanding production possibilities, an economy also enhances its consumption possibilities.

The potential output of an economy is determined by the quantity and quality of factors of production at its disposal. The factors of production are traditionally classified under four headings: land (resources found in the natural environment), labour (human resources), capital (output used for the production of further output) and entrepreneurship (the skills involved in bringing the other factors together to make valuable output).

The developed world has more and better quality factors of production available than the rest of the world. In other words, due to more favourable resource endowments, developed countries enjoy greater production possibilities than developing nations. This is illustrated in Figure 5.2 by means of production possibility frontiers. Assume initially that all resources are employed fully and efficiently, so that the diagrams can be analysed in terms of a choice between points on the frontier (and points inside it can be ignored). A poverty line is drawn on the frontier representing the volume of necessities that each country would have to produce in order to meet the basic needs of its population. It is assumed that the two countries have the same population, so that the poverty line occurs at the same level for each. Even if the developing country devotes all of its resources to producing necessities (point A), it still cannot meet all of the needs of its population. By contrast, a developed nation can meet all basic needs and enjoy a large number of luxury goods (any point in the range B to C).

Figure 5.2: The choice between necessities and luxuries

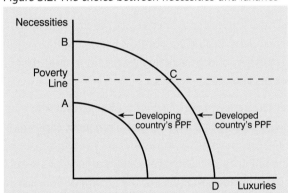

Economic growth can lift people out of poverty

Economic growth is represented by an outwards shift in the production possibility frontier. The importance of economic growth is readily understood in the context of Figure 5.2. If the frontier shifts far enough outwards, the developing country will be able to keep all of its population above the poverty line **and** enjoy luxury goods.

Even if such growth is attained, however, it does not follow that no-one will live in absolute poverty. For example, consider the PPF of the developed country. The political and economic structure of the country might be such that a choice in the range C to D is made. Some sections of society enjoy large quantities of luxury goods at the expense of others living in poverty. Accordingly, whether economic growth succeeds in lifting large numbers of people out of poverty depends largely on the distribution of income. Where there is extreme inequality, the benefits of growth may be concentrated in the hands of those who are already well off and little poverty reduction will occur.

The *growth elasticity of poverty* is an attempt to capture the extent to which growth results in poverty reduction. It is formulated on the same basis as other elasticity concepts such as price elasticity of demand:

Growth elasticity of poverty (GEP) = $\dfrac{\textbf{Percentage change in poverty}}{\textbf{Percentage change in national income}}$

A higher figure for growth elasticity of poverty indicates that poverty is more sensitive to increases in national income than where a lower figure exists. Current evidence suggests that the growth elasticity of poverty in Africa is around a third of that in the rest of the developing world (excluding China) as a result of the high degree of inequality found in Africa. For more detail, see the case study 'Growth and poverty reduction in Africa' below.

Growth and poverty reduction in Africa

Recent decades have seen spectacular progress in both growth and economic development in some regions of the world. Some middle-income countries have come to be termed emerging economies because of their rapid economic growth, including numerous newly industrialised countries in south-east Asia which now have western style economies. The *BRIC* economies (Brazil, Russia, India and China) have increasingly been the focus of attention for economists as their rapid growth and economic potential have provided both challenges and opportunities for developed economies. China is already the world's second largest economy. While rapid growth does not necessarily imply poverty reduction or an expansion in the range of economic and social choices for citizens, some impressive results seem to have been achieved. China, for example, grew by 10% a year for the three decades after it introduced market reforms in 1978, with a corresponding decrease in absolute poverty (on the internationally accepted World Bank measure of income below $1.25 per day) of more than 500 million people.

Until recently, however, there was little evidence of economic development in Sub-Saharan Africa. Indeed, as the number of people living in absolute poverty fell globally, the numbers continued to increase in Africa, with large numbers of people lacking the means to meet their basic needs, and the prevalence of disease and environmental problems.

During the past 10 years this picture has shown significant change, with African growth regarded as a bright spot in the world economy, even during the global economic crisis which began in 2007 and persisted for several years. The graph below shows Africa consistently achieving growth rates broadly in line with developing countries (excluding the rapidly growing China) as a whole. Excluding South Africa, which has faced a number of problems, the growth of Sub-Saharan Africa looks particularly strong.

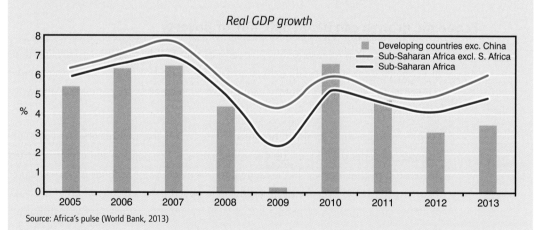

Real GDP growth

Source: Africa's pulse (World Bank, 2013)

Africa's population has continued to rise as it has grown and as a result the growth in its per capita GDP has not been as strong, but per capita GDP did grow in each of the ten years up to 2010 with the exception of 2009 which saw a small fall. Per capita GDP growth exceeded 3% in some years.

Between 1999 and 2010, Africa achieved a 9.5% point reduction in poverty as shown in the following graph. While this figure is close to the 10.8% point reduction in the rest of the developing world (excluding China), the fact that African poverty reduction has been fuelled by much larger increases in income than elsewhere hints that African growth has perhaps not been as productive in development terms. This appears to be because poverty reduction in Africa has been hindered by inequality, with the benefits of growth being very unevenly distributed. The *growth elasticity of poverty* in Africa is thought to be a third of that in the rest of the developing world (excluding China).

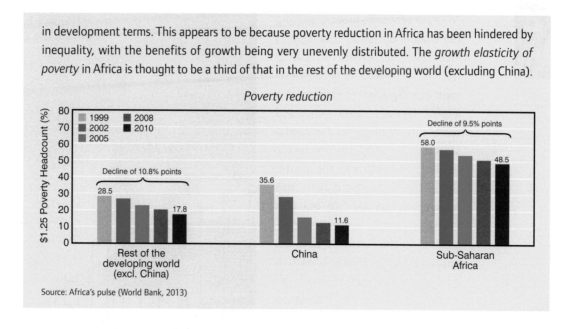

Source: Africa's pulse (World Bank, 2013)

The choice between investment and current consumption

To cause growth in potential output, it is necessary to sacrifice some consumption today. Resources which could have been used to make consumer goods and services must be diverted instead to enhancing the stock of resources available for future production. Investment in the future capacity of the economy therefore carries the *opportunity cost* of current consumption foregone.

The implications of this are particularly cruel for developing nations if it entails sacrificing consumption of basic necessities. This will be the case unless the sacrifice of current consumption comes from those living above the poverty line, either in the form of taxes paid to the government or through savings. It is likely to prove difficult to generate sufficient funds for investment from these sources. High rates of taxation are likely to cause the migration of the well off to other countries, while saving will only take place if sufficiently high interest rates are offered and there is little associated risk. Saving by residents of developing countries often takes place abroad, as the savers believe that there is less risk of the financial institutions of developed nations going bankrupt or because higher interest rates are available. This is known as *capital flight*.

Figure 5.3: The choice between investment and current consumption

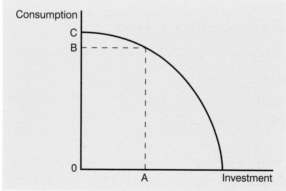

Figure 5.3 redraws the production possibility frontier to represent the choice between current consumption and investment. If we assume that OA of capital goods wear out (depreciate) each year, then this quantity of investment (known as *replacement investment*) must be undertaken each year just to maintain the current capital stock. This carries an opportunity cost of BC of current consumption. This sacrifice is sufficient to make sure that the production possibility frontier does not move inwards.

To cause economic growth, shifting the frontier outwards, total (*gross*) investment in excess of OA is required. The excess of gross investment over replacement investment is known as *net investment* and represents addition to the capital stock. *Ceteris paribus*, the greater the level of net investment, the greater the level of economic growth. This requires greater sacrifice but also increases further production possibilities in the future. It becomes apparent that economic growth is *cumulative* in nature. Current net investment makes more consumption *and* more investment simultaneously possible in the future. Due to the extra investment, the PPF will shift outwards again and the process continues.

Investment carries the opportunity cost of current consumption foregone.

The link between savings and investment: the Harrod-Domar growth model

The Harrod-Domar model was developed in the 1930s. The model suggests that high levels of savings are important because savings provide the funds which are borrowed for investment purposes. The economy's rate of growth therefore depends on the level of saving and the productivity of the investments which are undertaken. The productivity of investments can be summarised by the economy's capital-output ratio. If for example, $5 worth of capital equipment was needed to produce each $1 of annual output, a capital-output ratio of 5 to 1 would exist. A lower capital-output ratio is more favourable: a 4 to 1 ratio would indicate that only $4 of capital was needed to produce each $1 of output annually. The mathematics of the Harrod-Domar model are given in the following box (it would be possible to miss the box out while still gaining an understanding of the main points of the model).

The mathematics of the Harrod-Domar model

Mathematically, the Harrod-Domar model can be expressed as follows, where Δ denotes 'change in':

- Saving (S) is a given proportion (s) of national income (Y): $S = sY$

- Investment (I) is the change in the capital stock (ΔK): $I = \Delta K$

- Savings equal investment: $S = I$. It follows from above that: $sY = \Delta K$. We can rearrange this to give $Y = \Delta K/s$.

- The capital to output ratio (k) is defined as the ratio of the change in the capital stock to the change in the level of output (ΔY) that it causes: $k = \Delta K/\Delta Y$. We can rearrange this to give $\Delta Y = \Delta K/k$.

- Having derived expressions for both Y and ΔY, we can look at the determinants of the economy's growth rate. The growth rate can be defined simply as $\Delta Y/Y$. Using the relevant expressions we have: $\Delta Y/Y = (\Delta K/k)/(\Delta K/s)$. Cancelling the ΔK, which appears both on top and bottom, and rearranging: $\Delta Y/Y = s/k$.

In the following example, a developing country has a capital-output ratio of 4. With 4% saving, the economy then grows at a rate of 1% per year ($\Delta Y/Y = s/k = 4\%/4 = 1\%$). If the savings ratio can be increased to 12%, the economy can grow more rapidly at the annual rate of 3% ($\Delta Y/Y = s/k = 12\%/4 = 3\%$). In the event that a developing country could not achieve the level of saving desired, it could achieve higher levels of investment through injections of external finance (foreign aid, private foreign investment or borrowing from abroad). In the example above, suppose the country desired an economic growth rate of 3% but could only achieve a savings ratio of 4% (rather than the 12% needed). A 'savings gap' of 8% would then exist and could be filled by financial inflows from abroad.

Implications of the Harrod-Domar model and problems in applying it

The implications of the model are that economic growth can be brought about by:

● Higher levels of saving in order to boost investment.

● Increases in the productivity of factors of production (and thus a fall in the capital-output ratio). Particular attention here might be paid to the role of *technological advance*. Such advance is a major source of increased productivity. A brief consideration of the industrial revolution gives some idea of the importance of technology and the breathtaking technological advances in the past century have been a major driver of economic growth and a source of higher living standards in the developed world.

● Injections of external finance from other countries to offset any short fall in domestic saving.

However, there are a number of problems involved in applying the model. These include that:

● The desired level of savings may be very difficult to stimulate. Government policy may have little influence over the savings rate where absolute poverty exists and the first priority is consumption. Figure 5.4 shows that the majority of people in low and middle income countries do not save.

● Savings may be deposited with financial institutions abroad (*capital flight*).

● There may be problems that prevent the channelling of funds from those who wish to save to those who wish to invest. Figure 5.4 shows that the majority of saving in low income countries is not undertaken formally with banks. These savings may not be available to those who wish to borrow or invest.

● Offsetting any shortfall through external finance may bring its own problems. Aid may be 'tied', for example, and serve the objectives of the donor nation more than the recipient nation.

● If *diminishing marginal returns* to capital equipment exist, each successive unit of investment will be less productive and the capital-output ratio will rise.

● The productivity of investments may depend on complementary investments in other industries (see the sections immediately following this one).

Figure 5.4: Saving

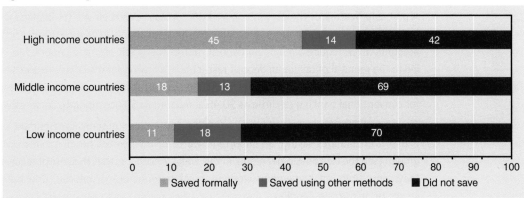

Source: World Bank, World Development Report 2014

Mobile phones can boost saving rates

The explosion of mobile phone use in poorer countries has been a major story in Development Economics in the past few years, especially in Sub-Saharan Africa. More people in the world have a mobile phone than have access to clean water supplies or sewerage. This is largely as a result of the operations of markets: In mobile phone provision it is relatively easy for firms to collect revenues which exceed costs, but this is not true in the water sector. Thus water is not likely to be provided privately and unless sufficient funding is available to the government to expand provision of water supplies it will not happen.

More people have mobile phones than toilets:

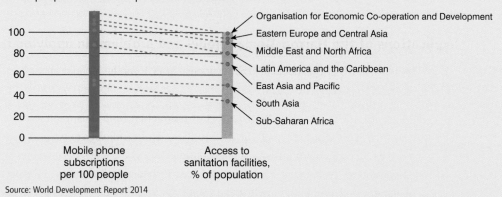

Source: World Development Report 2014

The extent to which telephones have become increasingly available in African countries is apparent from the following graph:

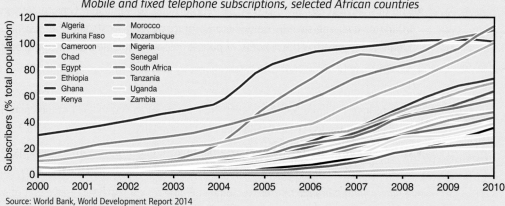

Mobile and fixed telephone subscriptions, selected African countries

Source: World Bank, World Development Report 2014

The increased availability of mobile technology is potentially very useful in development terms. Various studies have suggested that a 10% rise in mobile phone subscriptions in emerging markets leads to between a 0.6% and 1.2% increase in GDP. Improvements in business communications can be expected to lead to an increase in productivity.

A particular feature of the use of mobiles in Africa has been their use for banking. Mobile banking has made banking much more affordable to the poor than it was previously. Conventional bank accounts often require a minimum deposit, out of the reach of many people. Mobile banking has led to the removal of minimum deposit restrictions, allowing far more widespread access to banking services than previously. The cost per transaction undertaken by mobile banking is much lower than for conventional banking (as little as $0.46 compared to $3 according to some estimates).

The lower costs of mobile banking are useful in developmental terms for a number of reasons. One is that it encourages saving, an important source of investment funding, which can then lead to growth (see the Harrod-Domar model in this Unit). Another is that the cost of receiving remittances (payments from family members working in other countries) is reduced, providing an important source of investment funding.

Poverty traps as a constraint on development

Poverty may be self-perpetuating and hinder a country's economic development. Those who are poor are unable to afford to sacrifice current consumption in order to make savings. As suggested by the Harrod-Domar model, this serves to limit the funds available for investment, thus preventing economic growth from occurring. The net effect is that countries may become trapped in poverty.

The complementary nature of investments

Many investments can be viewed as complementary to one another. Investments made in capital equipment in particular industries, for example, are of limited use unless the increased output stimulated can be transported efficiently. This requires complementary investment in a transport network, in particular road and rail. Equally, the return to investment in such infrastructure depends on the use which is made of the network and hence on investments in particular industries. Another example is the backward and forward linkages that exist between industries. Any one industry is dependent on other industries for its raw materials (backward linkages) and to provide the market for its product (forward linkages). Investment in any one industry therefore provides benefits for its backward linkages from which it now demands more raw materials. Also, the success of the investment is dependent on finding a sufficient market from forward linkages for the increased output. The extra demand for raw materials from backward linkage industries might induce extra investment in these areas too; finding a market from forward linkages is likely to depend on how much investment has been undertaken there. Thus investments in linked industries are mutually reinforcing. The total benefit from any one investment exceeds the private return to the agent who undertakes the investment: investment carries *positive externalities*.

Balanced and unbalanced growth

Many economists argue that rapid economic growth is unlikely in developing countries unless investments can be coordinated. In a free market situation, low levels of investment are likely because of failure to take account of positive externalities and fear of not finding a market for output. This fear is likely to be particularly great where an economy is in the early stages of development. Added to the likely difficulty in obtaining funding for investment in countries where savings are low and financial institutions not well developed, this creates a recipe for stagnation and minimal growth. *Balanced growth* theorists therefore argue that it is essential that simultaneous expansion takes place in a wide range of industries, and that some government intervention is necessary to make this happen.

Amongst supporters of balanced growth theory, there is disagreement about the nature of this intervention. Some argue that the degree of coordination required can only be provided by wholesale central planning, in the form of a *command economy*. Others advocate increased taxes on high income earners, thus reducing the level of current consumption and providing investment funding which can be channelled by the government into coordinated investment projects. This can be achieved by the state undertaking investments directly (infrastructure investments and nationalised firms) and/or the use of *development banks*. Development banks are state owned and lend money for selected investment projects. These projects are not chosen on commercial criteria, but instead for their contribution to growth and development.

Unbalanced growth theorists often argue that it is not likely that sufficient resources will be available to permit widespread, coordinated investments to take place. This necessitates the prioritising of investment projects. Accordingly, an unbalancing of the economy must occur. Industries given priority for investment will grow faster than other areas of the economy.

It is argued that this unbalancing is actually beneficial, assuming that a fundamentally market based economy operates. Backward linkages (firms that supply raw materials) to the rapidly growing industries will find that they cannot keep pace with demand. Prices of the raw materials will rise, increasing profit margins in the industry and attracting market entry from new entrepreneurs. Investment in the backward linkage industries is therefore encouraged and supply of the raw materials extends. The forward linkages (firms that provide the market) for the rapidly growing industries will also find profit margins increased. They will now find that, due to surplus output in rapidly growing industries, their purchases are cheaper. Again, increased profit margins attract new entrepreneurs and extra investment. The role of the state is therefore limited to setting the process in motion, by deliberately encouraging rapid growth of certain industries. The chosen industries should be those with the greatest linkages with other areas of the economy. Direct state investment in these areas or the use of development banks are again the tools available.

The term economic structure refers to the different sectors that comprise an economy and to the balance of economic activity between those different sectors. Over recent decades, for example, the continuing economic development of the already highly developed United Kingdom has seen a reduction of manufacturing (secondary sector activity) and more output of services (tertiary sector).

Some of the main ways in which an economy can be divided up into sectors are covered in this unit.

Primary, secondary, tertiary and quaternary sectors

The distinction between these sectors may be made in terms of the following:

- **Primary sector.** This sector consists of agriculture and the extraction of raw materials (such as minerals, fossil fuels and wood) from the earth's natural environment.

- **Secondary sector.** The activity of this sector consists of combining raw materials to produce manufactured output. Manufactured output is all around us, including the clothes we are wearing and the furniture in the room.

- **Tertiary sector.** This is the service sector of the economy. Services are intangible and may be distinguished from the physical nature of the goods manufactured in the secondary sector. Services are diverse in nature including, for example, cleaning services, transportation, retailing and financial services.

- **Quaternary sector.** This sector of the economy delivers intellectual services. Although it would be possible to consider these simply as part of the tertiary sector, the term 'quaternary' has become more important as the role of technology and information has increased, especially in the developed world. This sector of the economy includes, amongst other things, education and consulting, scientific research and information technology.

Historically, the story of a country's economic development has tended to be in terms of progression through these sectors. This is in line with Rostow's stages of growth model (see Unit 7).

Many countries in Southeast Asia, such as Malaysia, South Korea and Singapore, have made rapid progress in recent decades through becoming highly competitive in manufacturing (secondary sector activity). Spectacular economic growth averaging almost 10% a year since 1978 has been achieved by China through a strategy of *industrialisation* grounded in its abundant supply of cheap labour. This has enabled China to become the world's second largest economy in terms of GDP. Industrialisation has drawn labour away from agriculture and into industry. The secondary sector has grown and the primary sector has shrunk as a proportion of GDP. China's rapid economic growth as this transition has occurred is shown in Figure 6.1.

Figure 6.1: China's GDP

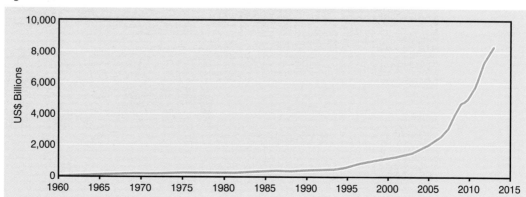

Source: tradingeconomics.com, World Bank Group

It is not always the case, however, that a nation's path to development involves gradual progress through the four sectors. A large contribution to India's growth over recent years has been made by its software industry (quaternary sector). India, in common with a number of other developing nations has derived income from the relocation of call centres for companies whose markets are primarily in the developed world (such as insurance companies and banks, for example). This expansion of tertiary sector activity has been made possible by virtually costless global communications, investment by the companies concerned and the availability of abundant, cheap and well-educated labour in the countries where the call centres are located. This is an aspect of the increasing *globalisation* of the world economy.

There are substantial regional variations in the nature of economic activity within individual economies. This includes nations that we would consider to be developed. Taking the UK as an example, much of the Midlands and the North have traditionally specialised in manufacturing, although this is less the case as time goes by. London is the centre of the UK's thriving financial service industry, while high technology, quaternary sector firms are disproportionately based in the South East. Many coastal towns specialise in tourism, while significant portions of Lincolnshire and Cambridgeshire fenland are given over to arable farming.

Rural and urban sectors

The rural sector of an economy refers to the economy of the countryside, while the urban sector consists of towns and cities. It is common for the rural sector to be dominated by agriculture (see, for example, the reference to Lincolnshire above). In many developing countries, agricultural activity will take place on a subsistence basis, with the produce being consumed by the family growing it, rather than it being traded. This is the case across large swathes of rural Africa. The urban sector tends to be the focus for manufacturing and industry.

The division between a rural agricultural sector and an urban industrial one is one aspect of the *dualism* present in many developing economies and may be linked also to a division in living standards, where the incomes of urban dwellers are often higher than those living in the countryside. This may provide an incentive for migration towards towns and cities (see the Lewis Model of structural change in Unit 7 and

In many developing countries agricultural activity is on a subsistence basis, such as here in south-east Asia.

also Unit 14 on migration). China again provides a good example, having a very sharp division indeed between the rural and urban sectors of its booming economy. The boom, at present, is largely benefiting the urban sector, as shown in Figure 6.2. Living standards are not always higher in urban areas, however. Many large cities in developing countries face problems with *unemployment* and slum settlements.

Economic development affects not just the pattern of labour usage, but land also. As an economy develops it is common for growing cities to spill over into previously rural areas.

Figure 6.2: Rural and urban incomes in China

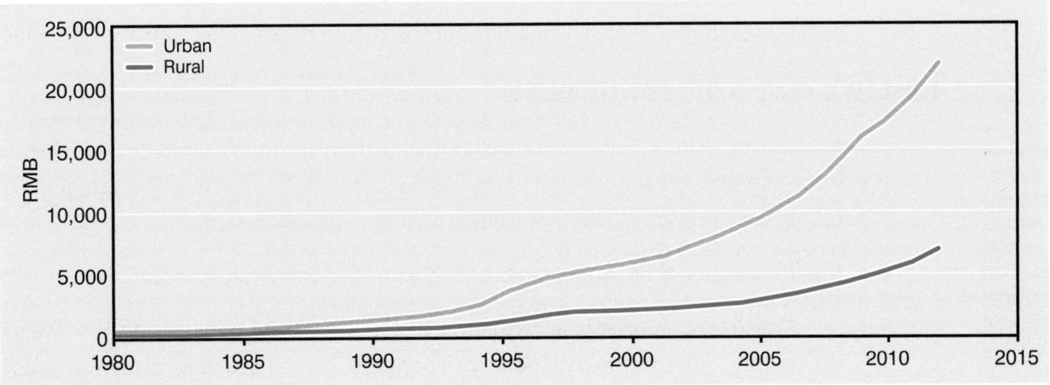

Source: CEIC and BCA Research

Formal and informal sectors

This is the distinction between registered and unregistered activity. The informal sector includes some activities that are illegal by their nature such as drug dealing. Prostitution often accounts for a significant proportion of the informal sector also. Other activity, although legal, may take place informally in order to avoid costs associated with registered activity, such as taxation or compliance with health and safety regulations. Street vending is common along with small permanent businesses such as restaurants.

Informal economic activity takes place in all economies. In developed nations one example of this is paying for services such as those of builders in cash and thus avoiding paying VAT. In the UK it is known that significant numbers of illegal immigrants work in agriculture and the hotel industry. The 20 cockle pickers who died when trapped by an incoming tide at Morecambe Bay in February 2004 were working illegally. In developing economies, informal sectors are generally much larger as a proportion of national income. One interesting aspect of this is that the official figures of developing nations may substantially under-report their national incomes, because of the omission of informal activity.

Traditional and modern sectors

Economic development is likely to see the reduction of traditional activities such as the growing of rice in India or tea in China. Both of these economies now have substantial modern sectors. The growth of the software industry in India is a good example of this, as are the manufactured and high technology exports of much of Southeast Asia.

This unit covers two models of development that both suggest that development consists of patterns of growth and change that are similar in all nations. Both deal with structural change (see Unit 6). Rostow's stages of growth model describes the process of development in five different stages, stages which are partly defined in terms of structural change. The Lewis Model is more explicitly about structural change and Lewis goes a step further than Rostow, in that his model explains how structural change may come about.

Rostow's stages of growth model

The American, Walt W. Rostow, suggested that a study of history demonstrates that developed countries have passed through a number of identifiable stages on the road to their current position. It was seen as necessary for developing countries to pass through these stages too.

In the first chapter of his work *Stages of Economic Growth*, Rostow wrote:

> "This book represents an economic historian's way of generalising the sweep of modern history… It is possible to identify all societies, in their economic dimensions, as lying within one of five categories: the traditional society, the pre-conditions for take-off into self-sustaining growth, the take-off, the drive to maturity and the age of high mass consumption… These stages are not merely descriptive. They are not merely a way of generalising certain factual observations about the sequence of development in modern societies. They have an inner logic and continuity… They constitute, in the end, both a theory about economic growth and a more general, if still highly partial, theory about modern history as a whole."

A number of factors characterising each stage of development can be identified:

Stage 1: Traditional society. Most economic activity takes place on a subsistence basis (output is not traded, but is consumed by those who produce it). Where trade does take place, it is likely to be the result of barter. Agriculture is the most important industry and production is labour intensive, using only limited quantities of capital.

Stage 2: The pre-conditions for take-off. Industries which extract raw materials from the natural environment begin to develop. Agriculture becomes more mechanised and more output is traded. Trade is encouraged by the growth of a transport system. Savings and investment grow, but to only around 5% of GDP. Some external funding is often needed to help a country progress to this stage.

Stage 3: Take-off. Industrialisation increases, with manufacturing growing and the numbers engaged in agriculture declining. Growth at this stage might be limited to one or two parts of the country and one or two industries. New political and social institutions are necessary to suit the new way of life. Savings and investment increase to around 10-15% of GDP, and are supplemented by external finance.

Stage 4: The drive to maturity. Growth should by now be self-sustaining and spreads to all parts of the country. Industry becomes more diverse and technology improves.

Stage 5: The age of high mass consumption. Output levels are high, providing the opportunity for mass consumption. The secondary sector of the economy produces more consumer durables than previously, while the tertiary sector grows. Accordingly, more people are employed in service industries than previously.

Recall from Unit 5 the conclusion of the Harrod-Domar model that economic growth requires greater levels of savings and/or improvements in technology. Both these insights are employed by Rostow in the model above. In particular, the preconditions and take-off stages are defined in terms of rates of saving and investment. The drive to maturity sees improvements in technology and hence reductions in the capital-output ratio.

The reader is likely to have noticed the implicit analogy with the flight of an aeroplane in Rostow's analysis. The traditional society could be likened to the aircraft when it is stationary on the runway; the economy is at a stand-still. The pre-conditions for the take-off of an aeroplane would include a fully working engine and the build up of sufficient speed. In much the same way, the economy requires infrastructure improvements and accelerating investment if it is to begin the growth process. With their respective pre-conditions satisfied, both the economy and the aeroplane are able to take-off. The economy eventually nears maturity with high levels of output, and the aeroplane approaches its cruising height. The final stage sees high mass consumption in the developed economy, and the aeroplane cruising at high altitude.

Figure 7.1: Rostow's stages of growth model

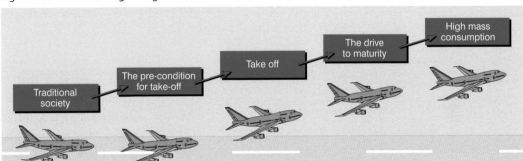

Criticisms of the stages of growth model

The stages of growth model has been criticised on a number of levels. It seems doubtful whether the development process is as simple as the model suggests. No-one would question the importance, indeed the necessity, of savings and investment. However, a high savings ratio might not prove sufficient to generate growth. Firstly, it is important that funds can be chanelled from savers to those who want to borrow for investment purposes. This seems to presuppose the existence of efficient financial intermediaries, such as those that exist in the developed world. Further, it is important that the conditions exist to allow investment to be productive. This will depend on the extent to which investment projects are coordinated. The productivity of investments in plant and machinery is dependent on complementary investments in infrastructure (such as road and transport facilities) and in the skills of management and the labour force (human capital).

Such criticisms are backed up by empirical evidence. Many countries in Africa and Asia remain at the traditional society stage, despite large injections of external finance. Those which have moved towards the take-off stage have found economic growth strangled by the need to repay huge debts incurred through international borrowing. This suggests that the investments undertaken have not been sufficiently productive to cover the interest levied on the borrowing.

Rostow suggested that the time taken to progress through the stages should diminish as countries learn from the experience of already developed nations. There is much empirical evidence that runs counter to this claim too, although the newly industrialised countries of East Asia (Singapore and Taiwan, for example) have grown very rapidly.

A whole body of literature has questioned whether the experience of countries that have achieved development actually conforms to Rostow's model. Just one amongst many examples is the work of Simon Kuznets. He argued that the now developed countries witnessed no significant rise in the rate of saving during their take-off stages.

The Lewis two-sector model

The work of W. Arthur Lewis views the economy as *dualistic* in nature, consisting of two sectors. These sectors are the rural subsistence sector and a modern urban industrial sector.

Initially, the majority of the population is employed in the rural subsistence sector. The implication of this is that labour will tend not to be very productive, because it is being combined with a fixed stock of (perhaps poor quality) land and capital equipment. This idea draws on the economic *law of diminishing marginal returns*. This states that as more of a variable factor of production is added to a given stock of fixed factors, there will come a point where the marginal product of the variable factor will decline. The marginal product is defined as the addition to output when one extra unit of the variable factor is added to the production process. The law of diminishing marginal returns recognises that labour inputs are complementary to inputs such as land and capital, and that there are consequent limits to the gains which can be made from specialisation as more labour is used. If ever increasing quantities of labour are employed, it is likely that the marginal product of labour will eventually decline to zero. A typical pattern for the marginal productivity of labour is shown in Figure 7.2:

Figure 7.2: The marginal productivity of labour

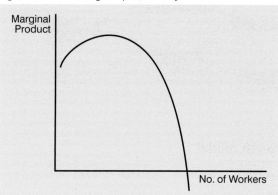

Lewis suggested that in less developed countries, employment in the rural sector of the economy was so great that many workers would have zero marginal productivity. He sought to explain the process by which this surplus labour might be transferred into the urban industrial sector, where it could be put to productive use. This would come about because the higher productivity of workers in the industrial sector would allow employers to offer higher wages than those in the rural sector; this would encourage workers to migrate to urban, industrialising areas. Lewis believed that an urban sector wage premium of about 30% over and above the rural wage would be sufficient to encourage such migration. Employers would be able to offer these higher wages while still enjoying profits. The reinvestment of these profits would then permit further expansion of output in the urban sector and the process of labour transfer would be able to continue. The process of industrial sector growth would be self-sustaining until all surplus rural sector labour had been transferred.

Rural to urban migration in practice

The Lewis model makes a number of debatable assumptions, not least that profits made by firms would be reinvested locally to permit further expansion of the urban sector and that any new capital created would generate jobs rather than replacing labour. These assumptions were crucial to explaining how rural to urban migration could be a continuing process.

While Lewis may not have been correct about the exact mechanism by which labour would be attracted from rural to urban areas, such migration has undoubtedly continued. In the past two decades, developing countries have urbanised on a massive scale (see Figure 7.3). The populations of developing countries are expected to grow by 1.2 billion people by 2030 with 96% of these extra people living in urbanised areas.

Migration to urban areas may be encouraged by a range of factors, not just employment prospects and higher wages, but also the higher standard of infrastructure and services available in cities, such as the wider availability of clean tap water. As the size of a city grows so too does the incentive for either domestic firms or multinational corporations to invest in the area to serve the larger market. The fact that poverty is

Migration to cities needs to be carefully managed to avoid environmental problems.

significantly lower in urban areas than rural areas has caused development organisations to encourage migration to cities although such migration needs to be carefully managed to avoid environmental problems such as those associated with slum settlements on the outskirts of cities.

Figure 7.3: Shifting of global population from rural to urban space

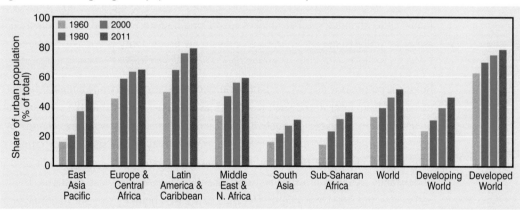

Source: World Bank

The neglect of agriculture in the pursuit of industrialisation

The role of agriculture in development has often been treated as of secondary importance to that of industrialisation. The Lewis model of structural change (Unit 7), for example, envisaged the role of rural agriculture merely as a source of labour to a growing urban industrial sector. As long as sufficient food was provided by the agricultural sector, then economic growth could proceed via industrialisation.

If the populations of developing nations were constant, this might prove a reasonable strategy. The transfer of surplus labour to the industrial sector would leave fewer participants in agricultural activity. The income corresponding to agricultural output would then be shared between fewer people and per capita income in this sector would rise. In practice, however, rapid population growth has seen absolute increases in the populations of rural communities despite the continued transfer of labour to now over-crowded cities. The neglect of agriculture as industrialisation has been pursued has consequently carried high cost. Constant inputs of land and capital equipment have been subject to diminishing marginal returns to labour as more workers are added to the production process. Agricultural output has not increased in line with the rural population and therefore per capita incomes have declined. Furthermore, the inability of many developing economies to produce enough food to feed their own growing populations has necessitated imports. This has contributed to balance of payments difficulties and imposed a constraint on economic growth.

The need for reform and obstacles to it

Farming in many developing nations, especially in Africa, is still largely at the subsistence level. Land is cultivated in small parcels by families using labour intensive methods, and produce is consumed by the family rather than traded. The families spend long hours on the land during planting and harvesting, but are often underemployed in between times. Low productivity is a major problem both for the farming families and for the national economy (see preceding section).

Reform is notoriously difficult, in part because of resistance to change amongst farmers themselves. Some observers have interpreted such resistance as irrational, given that the farmers would be the primary beneficiaries of increased productivity. We can make sense of resistance to change by understanding the risks associated with reform. The most important priority of the subsistence farmer is guaranteeing the survival of himself and his family. If this has so far been achieved by traditional methods which he understands well, this provides a strong incentive to continue these methods. The introduction of new techniques and new crops might offer the chance of a higher yield, but might also carry a higher risk of crop failure. This is particularly so in the early stages while the farmer is learning about the new techniques. Crop failure would threaten survival; reluctance to experiment is entirely understandable. Economists call such reluctance *risk aversion*. Even if the farmer is willing to pursue change, it is likely that affordable credit will not be available to meet initial investment costs.

Reform strategy

The aim of reform is to increase agricultural productivity. The agricultural sector needs to produce a surplus over and above what is necessary to guarantee the survival of those employed in this sector. This surplus can then be traded, feeding the rest of society and providing a higher standard of living for farmers. This surplus is likely to include a cash crop element. Cash crops are produced entirely for the market rather than for consumption. Common cash crops include tea, coffee, cocoa, cotton and rubber, many of which are produced primarily for export.

To overcome risk aversion on the part of farmers (see preceding section), reform strategy should include a number of strands. Farmers need information about new crops and the techniques for producing them. They also need access to credit and insurance facilities against crop failure. Development banks (see Unit 6) could play an important role in this regard. The preconditions for market trading should also be satisfied, and active marketing help is useful. A reform programme including these components changes the incentives to farmers and makes change more likely. Such policy contrasts sharply with past actions by many governments. It has been common for state agricultural marketing boards to be the sole purchasers of farm output at prices well below world market prices, with the aim of providing cheap food to other areas of society. This has limited the potential gains from reform and contributed to the reluctance of farmers to make changes. This is an example of *government failure*.

Cocoa is a common cash crop often produced primarily for export.

Diversification into mixed farming where staple crops are combined with cash crops, and perhaps simple animal husbandry, is sensible for a number of reasons. Because different crops are intensive in labour use at different times of the year, mixed farming lessens the problem of underemployment, maximising productivity and the farmer's tradable surplus. If mixed farming provides too great a demand on labour, small scale investments in labour saving devices (such as tractors and mechanical seeders) might prove possible. Cash crops are potentially lucrative for the farmer and improve the country's trading position if exported. Further, the impact of the failure of any single crop is minimised by the growing of other crops which might provide a substantial harvest. When substantial progress has been made, more costly but very productive innovations are likely to prove viable. These include investment projects to make the land more fertile, such as the installation of irrigation systems. It is shown in Figure 8.1 that per capita agricultural production has increased world-wide over the past fifty years. However, productivity has stagnated in Sub-Saharan Africa.

Figure 8.1: Changes in per capita agricultural production (1961-2005)

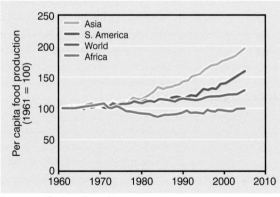

Source: www.foodsecurity.ac.uk

Capital intensive commercial farming

Agriculture in the developed world is characterised by high productivity on the back of capital-intensive, technologically advanced production methods. Such processes are not appropriate in the early stages of development for a number of reasons. Firstly, it makes sense in terms of development objectives to use labour-intensive production methods, given the abundant labour supply in most developing countries.

Further, capital-intensive methods lend themselves to large scale farming. This requires concentration of land ownership in the hands of fewer land owners. These land owners would be able to expect high returns from their land, but the relinquishing of land by small scale farmers would lower their living standards. In contrast to such a policy, it is often suggested that land reform is necessary in developing countries, with an enforced redistribution of land away from large landowners to those with only very small holdings of land or none at all. This will lend itself to the labour-intensive, mixed methods of farming described in the previous section. It will also make the distribution of income more equal and, arguably, more equitable.

A green revolution for Africa?

The problems referred to in this unit remain despite the 'green revolution', one of the key development successes in the latter part of the twentieth century. The use of high-yielding varieties of rice and wheat enabled food production in developing countries to triple over a thirty year period, cutting the number of rural poor in half, while the proportion of malnourished people dropped from 30% to18% (as reported by Pedro A. Sanchez and M.S. Swaminathan in *The Lancet*, Vol 365, January 29, 2005).

However, as suggested by Figure 8.1, Africa was left behind by this revolution. The reason for this lies largely in Africa's malnourished soils. Even high-yielding varieties struggle to grow in soil lacking sufficient nitrogen and phosphorus.

The former UN Secretary General, Kofi Annan, called for "a uniquely African green revolution for the 21st century". The UN Millennium Project Task Force on Hunger argues that this is possible on the basis of new farming techniques, such as the planting of trees that are capable of fixing atmospheric nitrogen in the soil. Fuel wood can also be harvested from such trees. The Task Force argues that the combination of such new approaches with conventional methods such as the use of chemical fertilisers and irrigation systems can dramatically raise agricultural productivity in Africa. It also calls for a small number of people in each village to be trained to deal with issues relating to agricultural productivity and markets, in addition to nutrition and health issues.

All this is argued to be necessary in order to achieve the Millennium Development Goal for hunger – reducing the proportion of people who suffer from hunger by half between 1990 and 2015. Such measures, of course, require financing, but may be examples of the speedy, cost-effective 'quick win' methods which characterise the planning to achieve the Millennium Development Goals.

Land reform and property rights in China

In China's economic boom, incomes in the urban industrial sector are growing much more rapidly than those amongst peasant farmers in the rural, agricultural sector. One reason for this is the issue surrounding the ownership of the land. In the 1980s, peasants were allocated tiny plots of land to farm as they wish, but were not given ownership of the land. Instead, the land was owned collectively by communes. Economic theory suggests that unless those farming the land actually own it they will have little incentive to invest in its productivity, because some or all of the gain from any investment would be likely to go to others. The argument is that secure property rights over the land need to be granted to individuals.

The situation has improved a little in recent years, with leases of up to 30 years to individual farmers. The long time scale should improve the incentive to invest because investments are likely to pay for themselves and yield a significant return within this time period. The incentive to invest is still not as strong as if the farmer actually owned the land, however. Also, the problem remains that the farmer may struggle to raise the finance for investment if he does not actually own the land, because he cannot use the land as security when taking out a loan.

The need for industrialisation

Both historical experience and economic theory suggest that structural change is a necessity for developing economies. The economic growth experienced on the path to development by today's First World countries was based on industrialisation and this was used by Rostow in his theory of growth (Unit 7). The Lewis model of structural change (Unit 7) argues the necessity of the transfer of labour from rural to urban areas, and hence from agriculture to industry. It also suggests the process by which this might happen. International dependence theory (see Unit 12) suggests that the current international division of labour is enforced by powerful nations, and that developing nations need to escape their enforced primary sector dependence. Free market theory (Unit 11) argues that as part of the global economic system, developing countries will receive inward investment. This will speed the process of industrialisation.

The costs of industrialisation

Because of the widely agreed link between industrialisation and economic growth, industrialisation is often an objective of development strategies. The choice to pursue industrialisation involves an opportunity cost, however, as all choices do. One element of this cost is the disruption that occurs to established ways of life, and often to cultural values. If free markets are to be used in the industrialisation process, for example, entrepreneurial values must be encouraged where they did not previously exist. Developing countries are often understandably reluctant to accept such change, especially those groups privileged by the old order. While it is not desirable to defend such privileges, it is important that development strategists balance the need for economic growth against other development objectives. If maximising economic growth entails undermining self-esteem it is likely to be worth accepting a lower growth rate. A second opportunity cost of concentrating on industrialisation has often been the neglect of agriculture, still of crucial importance to the vast majority of developing nations. The benefits of economic growth have been enjoyed by those in the industrial sector, while incomes for those in the agricultural sector have declined. Poverty is therefore increased in rural communities.

The choice between labour and capital intensive technologies

A low quantity and low quality capital stock is one of the factors that limits the potential output of developing nations. Investment in both physical and human capital is clearly an important part of industrialisation and economic growth, but we should recognise that capital and labour can be both substitutes and complements in the production process. In other words, physical capital can be *labour-saving* or *labour-using*. Labour-saving capital reduces the human input into the production process while labour-using capital increases it. Most developing countries have an abundant labour supply; unemployment is often high and underemployment common. Underemployment exists where workers are not employed on a full time basis. Many economists argue that *disguised unemployment* also exists, with surplus workers in the agricultural sector adding little or nothing to output through their endeavours. Unemployment indicates that an economy is operating within its production possibility frontier and imposes a human cost in terms of poverty for those unemployed and their families. It makes sense therefore for developing countries to pursue industrialisation through investment in labour-using capital.

Another way of putting this is to say that developing countries should seek to encourage those parts of the secondary sector that lend themselves to labour-intensive production methods. This makes sense both internally and from the perspective of finding new export markets. Once established, we would expect developing countries to be able to establish a *comparative advantage* in such areas, because the plentiful supply of labour ensures that this input is relatively cheap.

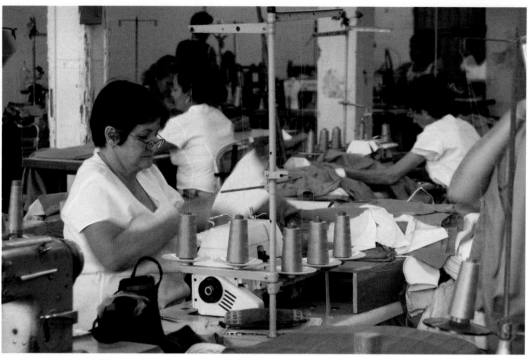

The first stage of industrialisation is to produce labour-intensive products such as clothing.

Schumacher's concept of intermediate technology

The economist E.F. Schumacher was wary of the possible costs of an industrialisation strategy that attempted to move in one step to an economic structure similar to the developed world. His primary concern was the importance of generating employment opportunities for the abundant labour force of developing countries.

In his book *Small is Beautiful*, Schumacher argues that generating employment should take precedence over enhancing labour productivity in the economy as a whole:

> "…it is necessary to emphasise that the primary need is workplaces, literally millions of workplaces. No one, of course, would suggest that output-per-man is not important; but the primary consideration cannot be to maximise output per man; it must be to maximise work opportunities for the unemployed and underemployed. For a poor man the chance to work is the greatest of all needs, and even poorly paid and relatively unproductive work is better than idleness."

Schumacher envisaged the employment of *intermediate technology*, more sophisticated than that currently employed in developing nations but much better suited to their needs than the industrial technology of the developed world. The technology would be more affordable to local entrepreneurs, not require extensive training to operate and be easier to repair. It would also be labour-intensive. He went on to write:

> "The intermediate technology would also fit much more smoothly into the relatively unsophisticated environment in which it is to be utilised. The equipment would be fairly simple and therefore understandable, suitable for maintenance and repair on the spot. Simple equipment is normally far less dependent on raw materials of great purity or exact specifications and much more adaptable to market fluctuations than highly sophisticated equipment. Men are more easily trained; supervision, control, and organisation are simpler; and there is far less vulnerability to unforeseen difficulties."

Import substitution

On the basis of the two previous sections, the likely first stage of an industrialisation strategy is to identify areas of production which lend themselves to labour-intensive production. Most of the goods which fall into this category are non-durable consumer goods, such as clothing, footwear, drinks and so on. Such goods enjoy a large demand in developing countries, a demand which is currently met by imports. The aim of an import substitution approach to industrialisation is to develop domestic firms which can produce some of the goods previously imported.

Large domestic demand does increase the chances of success for new firms, but so-called infant industries in developing countries are likely to struggle to compete with their established counterparts elsewhere. For this reason, the first stage of an import substitution programme is often accompanied by the use of substantial protectionist barriers. Developing countries are likely to use a system of quotas and tariffs in order to enable new firms to compete while they acquire expertise and expand output so as to gain economies of scale. It is desirable that protectionism should gradually be withdrawn, to expose domestic industry to the rigours of competition. In practice, this has often been obstructed by the political influence of entrepreneurs. It is unlikely that domestic industry will ever become fully efficient while such obstruction is allowed to succeed.

The approach to an import substitution programme can be selective in nature, with priority given to certain industries, or more comprehensive. This relates to the debate between balanced and unbalanced approaches to growth, covered in Unit 5. Each developing country will need to decide which strategy will deliver greatest benefit, given its own particular circumstances, although this itself is a difficult matter.

Economic growth due to import substitution of labour-intensive manufactured goods has a definite limit. Once all imports of goods of this type have been replaced by domestic production, the potential gains have been exhausted. Further growth then requires a change of strategy. One logical extension is expansion of production of these goods, to sell as exports on the international market (see next Section). Alternatively, the import substitution process might be expanded into more capital-intensive areas such as consumer durables.

Export promotion

Rather than focusing industrialisation on import substitution, an alternative is to concentrate on products which are to be exported. This strategy must clearly be orientated towards products for which there are high levels of demand from other nations. Possible roles for the government here include subsidy of the industries making such products. There may also be a need for the government to advertise in order to promote awareness of the nation's export potential.

Export promotion may be pursued from the start of an industrialisation strategy, or as a logical extension when the potential gains from import substitution begin to be exhausted.

Industrialisation in South East Asia

The economies of South and East Asia have frequently been cited as examples of success stories in the field of development economics.

Starting from a low per capita income basis in the early 1960s, many countries in this region achieved rapid improvements in their living standards. The per capita income of South Korea, for example, exceeded $100 per annum for the first time in 1963. By the early 1990s, South Korea and a number of other *high performance Asian economies* (HPAEs) had achieved per capita income levels to match those in the developed world. Singapore had climbed to ninth place in the world ranking of per capita income in 1994 (although it ranked fifteen places lower in terms of the United Nation's Human Development Index); in 1995 it came seventh.

(continued overleaf)

Much attention was paid to the causes of rapid economic growth amongst HPAEs. Both developing and developed countries searched for an 'Asian model' which could be applied elsewhere. In part, the difficulty in finding agreement on the causes reflected differences in ideology between economists. Economists disputed the relative roles of the market and planning processes. Pro-market economists observed with joy that public expenditure accounted for only a small percentage of economic activity in the region, while noting the ability of HPAEs to attract ideas, capital and know-how from outside. The importance of the private sector and global integration of economies was thus stressed. Their opponents drew attention to the responsibility taken by the state for strategic planning. Others concentrated on the role played by an industrious workforce, obedient to an authoritarian government. Differences amongst HPAEs themselves also made it difficult to agree on any shared characteristics which might constitute a model: any comparison between countries revealed wide differences in the role of the state, for example.

The complexity of the region's development process is captured by this attempt by the World Bank to summarise the causes of rapid growth in East Asia.

"The government intervened – systematically and through multiple channels – to foster development, and in some cases the development of specific industries. Policy interventions took many forms: targeting and subsidizing selected industries, keeping deposit rates low and maintaining ceilings on borrowing rates to increase profits and retained earnings, protecting domestic import substitutes, subsidising declining industries, establishing and financially supporting government banks, making public investments in applied research, establishing firm and industry specific export targets, developing export marketing institutions, and sharing information widely between public and private sectors. Some industries were promoted while others were not."

The suggestion that 'some industries were promoted while others were not' indicates an unbalanced approach to economic growth, as discussed in Unit 6. It is also clear that governments in the region pursued a strategy of industrialisation through import substitution. While policies were designed to encourage high rates of saving and investment, use of relatively labour intensive production methods enabled infant industries to compete internationally. Protectionist barriers to imports and subsidies to exporters aided this process, at least in the early stages. By the early 1990s, HPAEs had come to be classed as 'tiger economies' because of their high level of competitiveness in the increasingly global economy.

Inward and outward looking policies

Import substitution is an example of an inward looking policy: it focuses on a nation's domestic economy and the gains from development to be made therein. Export promotion is an example of an outward looking policy, seeking to foster development through international linkages.

Governments pursuing outward looking policies are likely to favour an 'open economy'. This will involve dismantling protectionist barriers such as tariffs. It may also involve removing obstacles to the international mobility of labour and openness to multinational corporations as a source of investment.

The case in favour of outward looking policies may be stated in terms of access to new sources of investment as well as access to the large global market and the economies of scale it can bring. The global economy is growing and generating higher incomes, especially for the residents of the developed world. This should serve to increase the size of export markets over time. There is also the notion that international competition acts as a discipline forcing domestic firms to become more efficient.

On the other side of the argument, there is concern that exposure to the full force of international competition may leave domestic firms unable to compete effectively. There are also concerns over the activities of multinational companies (see Unit 20). Increased international mobility of labour may involve developing countries losing talented individuals who have been trained using domestic resources, but will now use these skills in other nations (an external benefit to the recipient nation). This is the concept of a 'brain drain'. There are currently more African scientists and engineers working in the USA than Africa. However, employment opportunities for highly skilled workers are more lucrative in the developed world and 'worker remittances' (money sent home by those working in other countries) have become an increasingly important source of income for developing countries.

In many cases, an outward looking orientation has been forced upon developing nations by international institutions such as the IMF and World Bank (see the 'Washington consensus' in Unit 21). This is less the case than it once was. Development economists increasingly pay attention to individual national cultures and encourage 'ownership' of any development strategy by the developing country itself. From this perspective, one possible benefit of an inward looking strategy is the preservation of traditional ways of life. There is a concern that outward looking strategies may be part of an increased *globalisation* that reduces cultural differences and shows little sensitivity to the needs of the individuals affected.

Conclusion

Industrialisation is an important engine for economic growth and encouraging domestic production of labour-intensive manufactured goods is economically sensible for developing countries. Despite this, policy makers need to beware of potential conflicts with other development objectives and be mindful of the continuing importance of the primary sector of the economy.

Unit 10: Tourism

Tourism is an increasingly important source of income for developing nations, contributing a very substantial proportion of GDP for many of them (see Figure 10.1). It is the principal export for one-third of developing countries. Many governments are pursuing the promotion of tourism as an active development strategy, including putting public sector money into tourist marketing boards to increase awareness of their countries as tourist destinations, particularly amongst the citizens of rich, developed nations. Figure 10.2 shows that developing countries are expanding their share of the world tourism industry.

Figure 10.1: Ratio of travel exports to GDP in selected less developed countries, 2010 (percent)

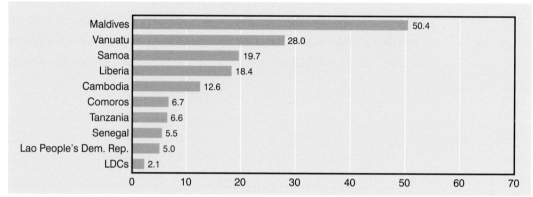

Source: World Bank

Figure 10.2: Developing economies are expanding their share in the world tourism industry

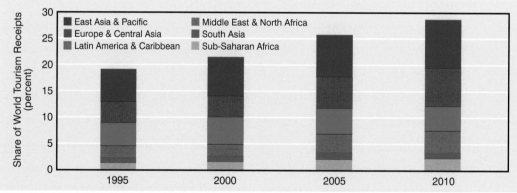

Source: World Bank, World Development Indicators 2010

Advantages of the promotion of tourism

Reasons for promoting tourism in developing countries include:

● The biggest assets of developing countries are often their environment (including areas of outstanding natural beauty) and their cultures. Tourism generates revenue from these assets.

● Modern communication devices such as the internet have made it possible to promote tourist destinations relatively cheaply. Increased levels of information have sparked increased interest in other cultures from residents of developed nations.

● Global prosperity is increasing, bringing with it higher income levels. Demand for tourist services is generally thought to be income elastic (demand responds more than proportionately to any given increase in income). Demand for tourism is therefore expected to continue to grow.

● Air travel has become cheaper over time, further boosting demand for tourism. For example, the eastern

European economies that are making the transition to market economies have enjoyed a boost to their tourist industries from cheap flights in Europe.

- Provision of tourist services is generally labour intensive. Some, but not all, of the labour used is relatively low skilled. Economic theory suggests that developing countries may enjoy a *comparative advantage* in labour intensive areas and tourism generates many employment opportunities. Each hotel room constructed is estimated to generate two jobs on average. The jobs created go disproportionately to vulnerable groups such as women and young people.

- Tourism creates injections into the circular flow of income from two sources. These are, firstly, the expenditure of the tourists themselves and, secondly, foreign direct investment (for example, investment by multinational hotel chains). These injections are likely to generate a multiple impact on domestic income as the recipients of the initial expenditure spend their income and create jobs and incomes for others. Aggregate demand for goods and services in the economy increases substantially.

- The infrastructure (for example, road networks) created to serve the tourist industry may generate external benefits for third parties involved in other sectors of the economy.

- Tourism may serve as part of a strategy of diversification of economic activity to avoid over reliance on any one sector. For example, at times when prices of agricultural output are low, the damage of this may be offset by income from tourism.

Patterns of tourism

In percentage terms, tourism is growing much faster in developing countries than in the developed world (see Figure 10.2).

In absolute terms, however, developed nations receive the bulk of tourist expenditure and are expected to *grow* faster in absolute terms in the coming years too. Table 10.1 details the ten countries where tourism is expected to grow fastest in relative terms (dominated by developing countries) and absolute terms (dominated by developed countries) until 2015. It also shows the nations expected to enjoy the fastest employment growth in tourism over this period. Two development phenomenons of recent years, India and China, feature prominently on all three lists.

Tourism in China has been growing at a very fast pace.

Table 10.1: Where is tourism projected to grow fastest, 2006-2015?

On a relative scale		On an absolute scale		On an employment scale	
Travel & Tourism Demand 2006-2015 *% Annualised Real Growth*		**Travel & Tourism Demand 2006-2015** *Growth in constant 1990 US$*		**Travel & Tourism Employment 2006-2015** *(extra 000s of jobs)*	
1. Montenegro	9.9	1. USA	569,330	1. China	13,986.7
2. China	9.2	2. China	305,554	2. USA	2,440.4
3. India	8.6	3. Germany	163,997	3. Mexico	2,434.3
4. Reunion	8.3	4. France	134,597	4. Indonesia	1,838.1
5. Croatia	7.8	5. Japan	124,938	5. India	1,812.2
6. Sudan	7.7	6. Spain	100,581	6. Brazil	1,433.4
7. Vietnam	7.7	7. UK	84,028	7. Spain	1,754.4
8. Laos	7.6	8. Canada	76,973	8. Pakistan	1,245.0
9. Czech Republic	7.5	9. India	57,327	9. Russian Fed.	1,213.7
10. Guadeloupe	7.2	10. Italy	55,259	10. Japan	927.7

Source: World Travel and Tourism Council: Progress and Priorities 2006-07

It is notable that some of the countries where tourism is expected to grow most rapidly in relative terms, such as Vietnam, are low income developing countries. What Table 10.1 does not show, however, is that the developing countries that at present gain the most from tourism are in fact middle income countries. An implication of this is that, other than South Africa and the north African countries of Tunisia and Morocco, the countries gaining most from tourism do not include any African countries.

Barriers preventing the growth of tourism

Not all developing countries are equally well placed to attract tourists. Barriers that might prevent the emergence of a successful tourist industry include:

- Climate.

- Lack of infrastructure and transportation links.

- Technological barriers (the capacity to use internet based booking systems is especially important).

- Lack of suitable labour. While some work in tourism is unskilled, this is not the case with all employment in the sector. Language skills are particularly important to a thriving tourist industry.

- Conflicts, including civil wars.

- Security issues and high crime rates.

Some of these factors may be overcome through sufficient investment. Governments wishing to promote tourism may pay particular attention to investment in road and rail networks, for example.

Negative externalities and other costs of tourism

Externalities are the effects that the actions of economic agents have on third parties. Externalities are received outside of the market place, in that those who suffer a negative externality are not compensated, while those who enjoy positive externalities do not have to pay for them.

The negative externalities caused in developing countries by tourism can be many and varied in nature, including:

- The effect of hotel and road construction on scenery and wildlife habitats.

- Air and noise pollution from construction.

- In countries with scarce water supplies, tourists are effectively in competition with local residents to consume the available water. Negative externalities from tourism may be lower food productivity as crops are inadequately watered, or disease as locals cannot access clean water. In 2013 the charity Tourism Concern found that tourists used 16 times as much water per head than locals in Zanzibar.

- Local cultures may suffer due to commercialisation. As well as directly affecting the lifestyles of local citizens, there is a danger that this commercialisation may ultimately reduce the attractiveness of the area as a tourist destination too.

- Litter dropped by visitors.

- Congestion on roads, especially in already very busy cities.

- Through increased air travel, tourism makes a substantial contribution to global warming. This, clearly, is a global issue, but global warming is likely to lead to flooding, more extreme weather conditions and increased difficulty in controlling disease in many developing countries.

Many of these externalities are not unique to tourism in developing countries. Residents of London, for example, are familiar with the externalities of litter dropped by tourists and additional congestion on roads and the underground system.

Other potential costs of tourism include the diversion of resources from other areas of the economy. The size of this cost depends on the use to which these resources would otherwise have been put. The opportunity cost of putting labour that would otherwise have been unemployed to work in the tourist industry is zero, for example, because the workers concerned were not previously producing any output. On the other hand, diverting those with high skill levels (those with management skills, for instance) into tourism may carry a high opportunity cost.

It may also be noted that the net gains from tourism may not be as large as they first appear. Much of the food and drink consumed by tourists has to be imported from abroad, while the profits generated by multinational hotel chains are enjoyed by the owners of those companies, not by local residents. Figure 10.3 shows the share of tourist spending reaching the poor for selected tourist activities in selected areas.

Figure 10.3: Share of tourist spending reaching the poor

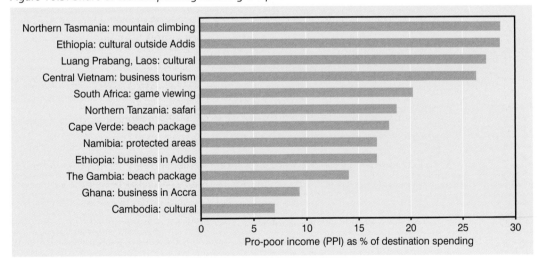

Source: Mitchell and Ashley, 2010

Should tourism be taxed?

The aim of encouraging tourism in developing countries is to generate a net social benefit after the social costs of tourism are taken into account. The social benefit consists of the private benefits enjoyed by those involved in the tourist industry added to any external benefits created. Similarly, social cost is equal to private cost added to the external cost.

A concern is that tourism may flourish because it is attractive on the basis of market incentives. If the private benefits of tourism exceed the private costs, there is money to be made and tourism is likely to increase. Given that tourism carries many negative externalities not accounted for by the market mechanism, however, things might look different when social benefits and costs are compared.

One approach to this problem is to impose taxes on businesses involved in the tourist industry. However, there are a number of problems with this. Economic theory suggests that any tax should be set equal to the size of the net negative externality generated by tourist activity, but externalities are notoriously difficult to attach a monetary value to. There is also the difficulty that areas imposing tourist taxes become more expensive to travel to relative to those where no such taxes are imposed. There is a likelihood that any developing country imposing a tourist tax would lose valuable tourist revenue.

Pro-poor tourism

Tourism can vary in its impact, with some forms of tourism being more effective at alleviating poverty than others. The pro-poor tourism movement promotes varieties of tourism that are effective in reducing poverty. A case study of pro-poor tourism in St. Lucia is given in the following box.

Pro-Poor Tourism in St Lucia

The people of St Lucia are taking part in a 'pro-poor tourism' project called the 'St Lucia Heritage Tourism Programme'. By developing a new branch of tourist attractions, the project could change the face of tourism on the whole island.

In the past, tourism in St Lucia has concentrated in certain areas where there are all-inclusive resorts owned by a few large operators and where cruise ship passengers come onshore for a brief visit. People living elsewhere on the island received few of the benefits of their visitors.

Working in partnership with local communities, the government is developing new cultural attractions that take advantage of the skills of poorer communities in farming, fishing, cooking and arts & crafts. By diversifying the island's attractions, the project hopes to tempt tourists out of their resorts, and encourage cruise ship passengers to stay on the island for longer. At the same time, the attractions promote the island's culture, so their visitors learn that there is more to St Lucia than sun, sea and sand.

One part of the project is a seafood extravaganza at Anse Le Raye. Here, tourists can sample the taste of St Lucia cuisine cooked by local chefs. Whilst their visitors enjoy the food, local communities can make a profit. Working together in planning these attractions strengthens community spirit too.

With more money in their pockets, local people are likely to spend more on other goods and services, giving the entire economy a boost But to ensure success in the long-term, EU funding of the project pays for training people in business and marketing skills. This way, local communities can develop high quality attractions that meet international health and safety standards. Also, these new skills enable local people to stand on their own two feet, giving them a better chance of competing with the more experienced tour operators even when the project funds have dried up.

Progress is slow as it takes time to change the well-established pattern of resort and cruise ship activities. Nevertheless, communities involved in the 'St Lucia Heritage Tourism Programme' are better off than before.

Source: www.globaleye.co.uk

Economic systems

Economics is concerned with the allocation of scarce factors of production or resources (land, labour, capital and enterprise) between competing uses. The available systems for deciding how scarce resources are used are:

The market system – The factors of production are privately owned. Consumers, firms and workers interact with each other, buying and selling in markets. It is assumed that, subject to constraints, consumers aim to maximise their own utility, firms aim to maximise profits and workers aim to maximise income. Market systems are responsive to consumer demand and it is largely this that dictates the pattern of output. If for instance, consumers demand more of a good, there is likely to be a temporary shortage. This causes the price to rise, rationing the available supply and signalling the shortage to producers, who now have an incentive to extend supply.

This is the price mechanism at work, or, by another name 'the invisible hand' referred to by Adam Smith. Without any central planning or coordination, the market directs resources to where they will produce the most utility (this is called allocative efficiency).

In a pure market system, the role of the government is simply to act as a supervisor of the system, for example by issuing notes and coins and through protecting rights to the ownership of factors of production and the goods and services produced ('property rights').

Central planning (Command economies) – Under this system, the factors of production are owned by the state on behalf of the people collectively. The state decides what is to be produced, how it is to be produced and for whom. The assumed motivation of the workforce is the collective good of society rather than individual gain.

The economies of the former Soviet Union were planned in this fashion, as was the Chinese economy until recently. Coordinating a large economy from the centre is difficult to accomplish and the plans did not always work well. For instance, some industries were not able to meet their output targets because they had not received raw materials from those that were meant to supply them. The composition of output inevitably reflected the priorities of the government. The Soviet Union ploughed many resources into the arms race as part of the 'cold war' with the West, but there were often long queues for bread.

Mixed economies – In reality, every economy in the world contains a mix of market activity and government intervention. The degree of this mix can be measured using government expenditure as a percentage of GDP. The trend over recent years has been for the role of government to be reduced. This is reflected in the trend towards privatisation of firms that were previously government owned. The economies of the former Soviet Union have made, or are in the process of making, the transition to being primarily market economies. China has achieved rapid economic growth since making market reforms.

The advantage of using markets in developing countries

- Governments may not make good choices concerning which projects to allocate scarce resources too. For example, government may fail to choose investment projects that are effective in reducing poverty for a number of reasons. These include lack of information about the effects of the investment, conflicting political priorities and corruption (all of which are sources of *government failure*).

- Where governments are responsible for production, waste in the production process is common (technical or 'X' inefficiency). This is because governments lack the motive of profit that encourages private firms to cut waste in order to reduce costs. This was a significant motivation for privatisation in developed countries like the UK (where water, gas, electricity, telecommunications, coal, steel and the railways were

all privatised in the 1980s and 1990s). It also applies to developing countries. Cutting waste raises the output produced from any given quantity of resources.

- The total level of investment may be higher when it is motivated by the opportunity to make profits in a market economy where enterprise is encouraged. This may include foreign direct investment (FDI) undertaken by multinational companies.

Overall, it is thought that because markets reward economically beneficial behaviour (such as working and investing), they are likely to function well. Experience suggests that market based economies tend to grow faster than centrally planned economies.

Problems of encouraging market activity in developing countries

The pre-conditions necessary for the effective functioning of markets may not be in place in many developing countries. These include:

- **Adequate infrastructure.** Good roads and a well-functioning transport system are vital if goods are to be transported to their final destination in a market system. Participation in a global market system also requires good airports and shipping ports. Good communications systems such as telephone networks and the internet are needed in order for buyers and sellers to coordinate market activity. Such infrastructure is clearly lacking in many developing countries at present, and it is difficult to see how the market would provide it. Private firms will not build roads unless they can make profits from them. This will not be possible until a flourishing market system is already up and running: good roads are a precondition for market activity, but the roads will not be built unless there is already a flourishing market! Before private firms would build roads it would also be necessary for them to ensure that they could prevent those who have not paid using the roads (the 'free-rider' problem) and even then enough roads may not be built because private individuals cannot be expected to take into account the positive externalities associated with road building. Further still, the return to investing in construction of any one road depends on a large number of other roads being built to form a network. All in all, it looks likely that there would be market failure if the private sector were left to build the infrastructure for a market system and so there is a clear role for the government here.

- **Well-functioning financial institutions.** In a market economy, investment depends on financial intermediaries such as banks channelling funds from savers to those who wish to borrow for investment purposes. Without such institutions, it is unlikely that a market economy will flourish. The state may need to create and maintain a banking system.

- **Protection of property rights.** A strong, well functioning legal system is required. Entrepreneurs are only likely to invest in what they legally own and when they are confident that the law will protect their ownership. The rewards of investment are reaped in the future, whereas the sacrifice required to make the investment occurs at the present point in time. This sacrifice will not be made unless entrepreneurs have reasonable confidence that the law will protect their rights to the benefit of the investment.

- **Entrepreneurial culture.** The incentive of individual gain may clash with the cultures of many developing countries. Even if there is no such clash, traditional ways of life may make it difficult for market activity to take hold. Subsistence farming, for example, is undertaken for the gain of the individual farmer and his family but where subsistence farming has always been the norm this may be a barrier to market activity.

- **Stability.** Markets function well when there is a relatively stable macroeconomic climate. This means, amongst other things, that inflation needs to be low and fairly predictable. This is because the price mechanism as a system of resource allocation relies on producers reading price signals. Changes in the relative prices of different goods can be very difficult to interpret when inflation is rampant. Further, high levels of inflation are undesirable because they erode faith in the ability of the currency to act as a 'store of value' or, in other words, a vehicle for saving. If individuals are reluctant to save, investment is likely to be low. Avoiding inflation means that governments should avoid running big budget deficits (where government spending exceeds taxation revenue). Running deficits may be entirely understandable in economies where poverty is widespread, but such deficits create a temptation for governments to print money and this is inflationary. A relatively stable exchange rate is important to the functioning of a market economy too. Wild fluctuations of exchange rates increase the risks involved in international trade and therefore discourage importing and exporting. Programmes to force governments to adopt tight fiscal and monetary policies to create stability have often been implemented by international organisations such as the IMF (see Unit 21).

Besides the possible absence of these pre-conditions for the effective functioning of markets there may be other problems in using markets in developing countries too. These include:

- **The sudden introduction of market activity can cause problems.** Sudden privatisation of things that have always been done by the state can cause serious dislocation. For example, in countries where the government has always been responsible for rice imports in order to bridge gaps between domestic production and consumption, turning this activity over to private individuals and firms may be a recipe for disaster. There may be factors that prevent the private sector from importing such as the high risks associated with fluctuating prices in a market system. The result may be mass starvation. It cannot be assumed that privatisation in the developing world will work as effectively as it has done in countries with already developed economies.

Some dislocation is almost an inevitable feature when an economy that has previously been planned on a wholesale basis makes the transition to a market economy. This was very much the experience of the Eastern European countries that began this transition in the late 1980s and the 1990s, although economic growth in the economies in transition is now strong. Please see the separate box for more details.

Transition and development in Eastern Europe

The transformation of Eastern European economies to market economies was never likely to be painless. Early attempts at partial reform had proved difficult and the initial impact of the rapid introduction of a market system known as 'shock therapy' was difficult to bear too. The drive for efficiency led to many workers being made redundant. Also, the end of state allocation of resources meant that firms no longer had guaranteed access to factors of production; nor could they be sure of finding a market for their own product. Each firm now needed to create its own forward and backward linkages. Those firms that struggled to do so found their survival threatened, with consequent losses of output and jobs. In such an uncertain climate, firms were understandably reluctant to invest. This in turn generated output losses and unemployment in the capital goods industry. Each reduction in output and employment levels resulted in multiplier effects that further damaged economic performance. Meanwhile, reductions in supply were accompanied by an explosion of demand. As part of the price fixing regime of the command economy, demand had been suppressed. The removal of such suppression boosted demand considerably, resulting in high levels of inflation.

The economic dislocation described above was inevitable. Output levels in some economies in transition collapsed, as in Latvia which experienced a fall of 34.9% in 1992. Such problems were expected to be relatively short term where the shock therapy approach was used. For example, Poland experienced rampant inflation and an 11.6% reduction in output in 1990 but output began to recover in 1992. Inflation was still at 43%, but falling rapidly. Improvements in both variables have continued since this time. Where reform has been slower, the results have been more damaging. The Ukraine is a prime example, its poor economic performance between 1991 and 1999 being confirmed by the data in the table. The table shows that output levels had begun to recover in a number of transitional economies by 1997.

(continued overleaf)

Countries in transition: annual percentage change in real GDP

Country	1990	1991	1992	1993	1994	1995	1996	1997	1998	1999	2000
Bulgaria	-9.1	-11.7	-7.3	-1.5	1.8	2.9	-10.1	-7.0	3.5	2.4	4.8
Croatia	-7.1	-21.1	-11.7	-8.0	5.9	6.8	5.9	6.8	2.5	-0.3	3.6
Czech Republic	-1.2	-11.5	-3.3	0.1	2.2	5.9	4.8	-1.0	-2.2	-0.2	3.1
Estonia	-8.1	-13.6	-14.2	-8.5	-2.0	4.3	3.9	10.6	4.7	-1.1	6.4
Hungary	-3.5	-11.9	-3.1	-0.6	2.9	1.5	1.3	4.6	4.9	4.5	5.2
Latvia	-3.5	-10.4	-34.9	-15.0	0.8	-1.0	3.3	8.6	3.9	0.1	6.6
Lithuania	-6.9	-5.7	-21.3	-16.2	-9.8	3.3	4.7	7.3	5.1	-4.2	2.9
Poland	-11.6	-7.0	2.6	3.8	5.2	7.0	6.0	6.8	4.8	4.1	4.1
Romania	-5.6	-12.9	-8.8	1.5	3.9	7.1	3.9	-6.1	-5.4	-3.2	1.6
Russia	-3.0	-5.0	-14.5	-8.7	-12.7	-4.1	-3.4	0.9	-4.6	3.2	8.3
Slovakia	-2.5	-14.6	-6.5	-3.7	4.9	6.7	6.2	6.2	4.1	1.9	2.2
Slovenia	-4.7	-8.9	-5.5	2.8	5.3	4.1	3.5	4.6	3.8	4.9	*
Ukraine	13.0	-8.7	-9.9	-14.2	-22.9	-12.2	-10.0	-3.0	-1.9	-0.4	6.0

Source: The Economist Newspaper Limited, 1990-98; World Economic and Social Survey 2000-2001   *Data unavailable

The improvement in the outlook for economies in transition has continued since this time, despite a blip during the global recession, as shown by the following data:

	'01	'02	'03	'04	'05	'06	'07	'08	'09	'10	'11	'12*	'13*	'14*
Economies in transition, growth of output (%)	5.7	5.1	7.1	7.7	6.5	8.0	8.4	8.0	-6.6	4.1	4.5	3.2	3.1	3.7

Source: UN World Economic Situation & Prospects, various years including 2013   *Forecast

Growth in transition economies is now outstripping global economic growth. There are a number of other development implications of the transition to a market economy. These include that the change has been associated with greater political and economic freedoms, expanding the range of choices available to citizens. Also, the distribution of income and wealth is changing substantially. To some, this is both necessary and desirable. To others, it is viewed as anti-developmental because of the negative impact on those who neither own physical capital nor possess high levels of human capital. Indeed, it could be argued that the concept of greater economic choice is hardly relevant to those now experiencing low incomes.

- **Market failure due to externalities.** Market activity is based on the private costs and benefits of the buyers and sellers involved, who do not have an incentive to take into account the effects on third parties known as *externalities*. Government intervention may be necessary to correct for externalities, especially significant externalities such as pollution and environmental degradation. Governments in developing countries where market activity is only just taking hold may not have the necessary experience to intervene effectively.

- **Market failure in the case of merit goods, public goods and other missing markets.** There are some goods for which markets tend not to work well. *Merit goods* such as education and healthcare are under-provided in free markets and there may be no market for *public goods* such as national defence at all. In the early stages of the take-off of market activity there may be many other goods for which there is no market (*missing markets*). Significant amongst these may be insurance markets. The possibility of insuring against risks makes it much more likely that those risks will be taken and market economies depend on the acceptance of the risks associated with investment, for example. There are clear roles for government intervention here, but question marks over how effective that intervention might be. In particular, funding for some types of intervention is an issue. In development terms, free education and health care for all are desirable but not within the reach of governments if taxation revenues are low and they are restrained from running budget deficits in order to create a stable economic climate. Aid is likely to be necessary to bridge the gap.

- **Market activity tends to lead to inequality.** In a market economy, the distribution of income tends to be very unequal. It is partly this that generates the incentives that enable markets to deliver high levels of output, but it also means that those with few skills receive very low incomes. This is likely to be a concern associated with the widespread use of markets in developing economies. Financially stretched governments are unlikely to be in a position to provide welfare systems to lessen this inequality.

- **Corruption in government is widespread in many developing countries.** This may impede the functioning of a market economy. Please see the box on corruption as a constraint on development.

Corruption as a constraint on development

There are many ways in which corruption can hinder economic development, these include:

- Money may be embezzled by government officials rather than being spent on public services or investment. This may include money received as aid from other nations. Such embezzlement is likely to discourage aid donations. The money embezzled also leaks from the circular flow of income, in many cases to bank accounts and financial investments in other countries.

- It is unlikely that scarce resources will be allocated efficiently when they are allocated on the basis of bribes to government officials.

- Corruption may include the seizure of property. As explained in previous sections, market incentives cannot function properly in the absence of secure property rights.

- Governments may spend money in ways that further their own political ends, for example, the stock-piling of weapons.

Because corruption reduces the resources available for public sector investment and also interferes with market incentives, economies with high levels of corruption tend to experience low levels of economic growth.

The role of government

This unit has suggested a number of roles for government, even where markets are to be widely used in the development process. These roles include protecting property rights and creating a stable macroeconomic climate. They also include creating other pre-conditions for market activity such as adequate infrastructure and financial markets, such as banking. Further, government action may be necessary to overcome a variety of market failures.

This is a minimal interpretation of the role of government. However, even where market activity is encouraged, development planning by national and international governmental institutions still has a role to play. An example is the planning by the United Nations to put into place the measures they believe necessary to achieve the Millennium Development Goals (see Unit 1). This planning includes deliberate targeting of 'quick win' development measures such as anti-malarial medicine and the abolition of school fees. Note that the UN recognises the importance of markets and indeed calls for the identification of nations that deserve large increases in funding as a reward for 'good governance'. This good governance certainly implies a lack of corruption, but also entails creating the conditions in which market activity can flourish. Awarding aid only to nations with 'good governance' helps to ensure that the money will be effectively spent. It also gives other governments an incentive to eliminate corruption.

Dependency theory

International dependence models stress external rather than internal causes of underdevelopment, in contrast to the models examined earlier in Section B. They are *dualistic*, in the sense that they draw on the idea of a sharp division between rich and poor nations. The hypothesis is that the division is lasting and the gap is likely to widen, not narrow, over time. The notion that the wealth of developed nations might 'trickle down' to developing nations (perhaps through trading relationships, for example) is rejected. In fact, most dependence models argue that developed countries cause a state of under development in poor nations. Theories differ as to whether the richer countries intend this to be so or not; but they share a view of the international economic system in which the developed countries are at the centre and poorer nations on the *periphery*, dominated by countries at the centre.

Ways in which developed countries may have caused the problems of developing nations include:

- **Colonialism.** Many economists believe that the primary causes of today's unequal distribution of world income and wealth can be traced back to colonialism, when the colonies were forced to concentrate on the production of primary produce. The resulting international division of labour largely still exists today. In the meantime, however, the terms of trade of developing countries have worsened (see Unit 4 for more details). Thus, while developed nations do not necessarily deliberately perpetuate this situation, it can still be attributed to their past actions.

- **Poor advice.** Some economists believe that inappropriate economic advice given by economists of developed nations is to blame for the problems still facing many developing nations. This might be well-meaning, but has failed to take account of the particular conditions existing in poor nations. The advice to fill the savings gap (see Unit 5) with injections of external finance is a case in point. In many developing countries, conditions were not such as to allow investments to be productive enough to earn the currency needed to make repayments on loans. The international debt crisis, imposing severe restraints on economic growth in poor nations, resulted. A more pessimistic interpretation of the debt crisis is that it was deliberately caused by developed nations in order to help them further their dominance of the international economic system.

- **Deliberate intent.** Other models observe that a dualistic situation exists within developing nations, as well as internationally. A small, ruling class in poorer nations benefits from maintaining the current position. This group, enjoying high incomes and a privileged social position, might include landowners, merchants, government officials, and trade unionists amongst others. The benefits enjoyed by this group are derived from the international capitalist system, in which they serve their masters from the developed nations. The power of developed nations is exercised by institutions such as multinational corporations, the World Bank and International Monetary Fund (IMF). Ruling class members in poorer nations are rewarded by these institutions for keeping wages and prices of raw materials low and discouraging diversification into industries in which the developed countries specialise. This model is *Marxist* in nature and attributes intent on the part of the developed world to dominate poorer countries, regardless of the public message given out by institutions like the IMF.

A common interest

The dependency theory discussed in the previous section is rather pessimistic. It treats developed countries, either deliberately or otherwise, as the cause of the problems of developing nations. It is easy to take the view that the interests of rich developed countries and those of developing nations are in opposition to one another, and that the gain of one is the loss of another (this is sometimes termed a 'zero sum game'). For instance, it could be argued that developed countries exploit cheap labour in developing nations in

Diseases spread more easily in developing countries and can impact the developed world.

order to make the goods they import from those nations more affordable: Higher wages would improve living standards in developing countries, but would make it impossible to buy a pair of jeans for £5 in the UK, as it is possible to do at present.

However, other takes on the relationship between developed and developing countries currently hold sway. These hold that not only does the developed world have a moral duty to help improve living standards in developing nations, but that it is in the interests of all countries that developing nations should escape poverty.

Possible reasons for this include:

- As developing countries achieve economic growth, the number of consumers in the global market grows, increasing the export potential of developed nations.

- Further incidences of famine in developing nations, especially Africa, will trigger mass migration creating problems for countries attempting to absorb large and sudden influxes of immigrants.

- Poor countries with poor governance have often proved to be breeding grounds for terrorism. For example, Al Qaeda, guilty of the September 11th attacks, has used Afghanistan for training purposes.

- Disease spreads more easily in developing countries because of the lack of facilities to contain it. Some of these diseases have the potential to cause widespread suffering in developed nations.

- Improving living standards in developing nations to the extent that they are self-supporting would reduce the need for aid payments from the developed world.

This view of the relationship between the developed and developing world is at the heart of the current drive to achieve the Millennium Development Goals (see Unit 1). It is worth noting that Goal number 8 is to "Build a global partnership for development". In 2005, the UK government-instigated Commission for Africa published its report entitled *Our Common Interest*.

Population and the environment

Unit 13: Population growth

Past and future population growth

During the twentieth century, the world's population grew rapidly, and at an increasing rate. This is in comparison to slow growth throughout the rest of history. Very rapid growth is forecast to continue during the first half of the twenty-first century (see Figure 13.1).

Figure 13.1: World population growth 1950-2050

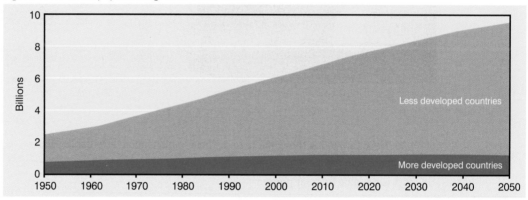

Source: United Nations, *World Population Prospects, The 2012 Revision* (medium variant)

In the four decades between 1950 and 1990, the world's population more than doubled to approximately 5.3 billion people. Most of the population growth in the early 21st century is expected to take place in developing countries, as shown by Figure 13.1. This growth will occur mainly in urban areas. Although not shown individually by the diagram, the populations of Asia and Africa are expected to grow especially rapidly.

The global population will approach stability, with a probable total of around 10 billion people, in the second half of the 21st century.

The demographic transition

Rapid world population growth is caused by birth rates exceeding death rates for the world as a whole. This is not the case in all nations, however. In particular, population growth is close to zero in developed nations. In the developed world, birth rates and death rates are now approximately equal. The term *demographic transition* is used to describe the experience of developed countries on the path to achieving stable populations. It is usually described in terms of three stages:

Stage 1: Population growth was slow. High birth rates were accompanied by high death rates. High death rates were caused by factors such as poor diet, standards of sanitation, health care and periodic wars and bouts of disease.

Stage 2: The population grew rapidly, because birth rates remained high as death rates fell. Improvements in factors such as diet and health care caused a rising life expectancy.

Stage 3: Birth rates began to decline, eventually reaching similar levels to death rates. The population stabilises.

Thus the experience of now developed countries suggests that both death and birth rates decline as a country becomes more developed, but birth rates take longer than death rates to respond to the development progress.

Dependency ratios

The dependency ratio is the ratio of dependants (economically inactive people) to the economically active. Dependants include children below working age and old age pensioners. Other dependants are of a working age, but are still not economically active. These include students and housewives. A high dependency ratio is seen as a problem economically because it makes it more difficult for a country to attain a high per capita income. For example, suppose that two countries have the same working population and available quantities of all other factors of production. If the two countries operate with the same degree of efficiency, they will achieve the same total output (and hence income). Country A, however, has more dependants than Country B and therefore a higher dependency ratio. Given that Country A has a higher population, its per capita income will be lower than that of Country B.

Population growth as a constraint on development

Most developing countries have been passing through stage 2 of the demographic transition, with rapidly growing populations. This can hinder the development process. Although total GDP may be rising it is likely that per capita GDP will fall due to increasing population. This is especially likely because the dependency ratio tends to be high during stage 2 of the transition. The population increases at this stage because the death rate slows down, while the birth rate is still high. So the addition to the population is in the form of children and old people, who need to be supported by those able to work.

Population growth also has environmental consequences. In developing countries, these have included the degradation of farm lands and deforestation. These and other environmental problems associated with development are discussed in detail in Unit 15.

It seems to be in the interests of both developing and developed nations to curtail population growth. Developed nations are keenly aware that environmental problems have global consequences. However, critics argue that the main problem is not developing country population growth, but excessive consumption demands in developed nations. A child born into the developed world has sixteen times the effect of an additional child in the developing world in terms of depletion of the world's scarce resources.

A window of opportunity

Most developing countries have now entered stage 3 of the demographic transition. Stage 3 is, initially, much more favourable economically. Low birth rates reduce the proportion of the population which is below working age. The last generation to be born in the era of high birth rates progresses to form a large workforce. This is good both for current living standards and the future, because the middle aged tend to save more than other sectors of the population. This provides the funding for investment (see the Harrod-Domar model in Unit 5). The early part of stage 3 is sometimes called the 'demographic window' because of the opportunities it offers. Figure 13.2 shows falling dependency ratios for developing countries in the early 21st century. The transition through stage 2 and into stage 3 took place in the space of a single generation for some newly industrialised East Asian countries. Their rapid economic development is attributed by many economists to favourable demography, at least in part. Others counter with the view that favourable demography is caused by economic development rather than vice versa. The two could be viewed as mutually reinforcing.

It is vital that countries in the early part of stage 3 take full advantage of the demographic window and save substantially to provide for the future. This is because the dependency ratio will rise again as the large middle aged group reaches old age. This is much the problem facing developed nations over the next few decades (see high income OECD countries in Figure 13.2), a problem severe enough to be known as the 'demographic timebomb'. This is caused to some extent by special factors. The end of World War II saw a period of extremely high birth rates (the 'baby boom generation') but birth rates slowed dramatically as sophisticated modern birth control methods became available. The baby boom generation reaches old age in the near future, placing a restraint on per capita income growth. Other problems include a crisis in state pension funding, given that it is common for the taxation revenue from the current working generation to fund the pensions of the previous generation, now retired.

Figure 13.2: Dependency ratios on the decline – for a while

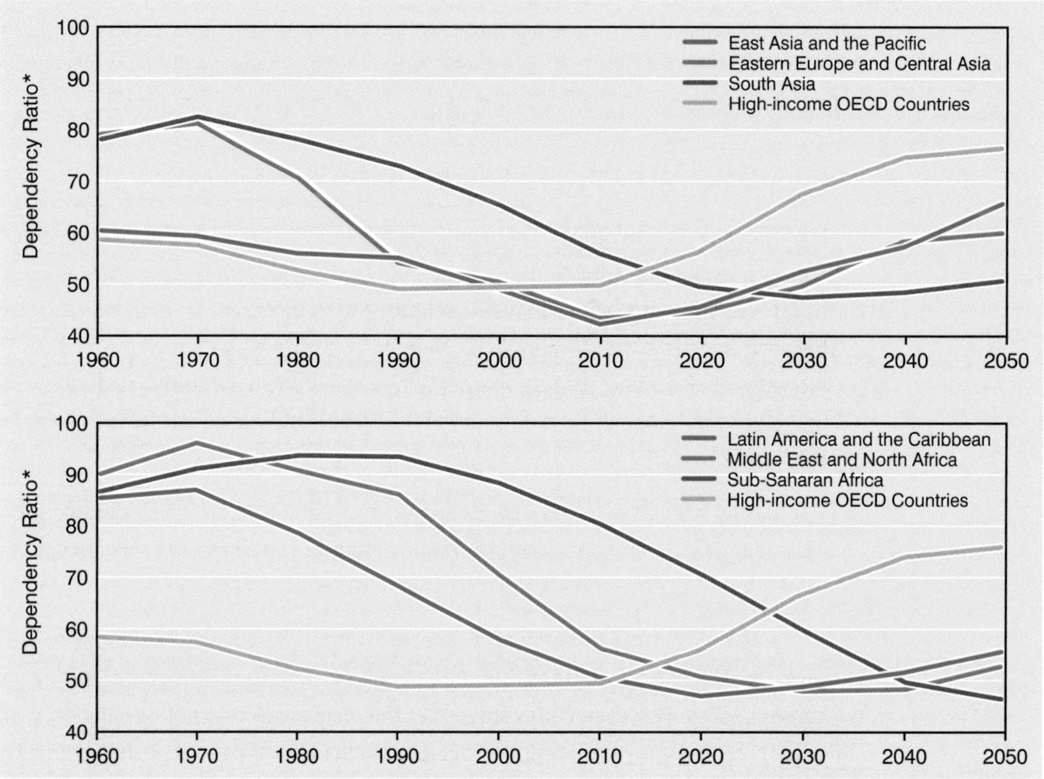

Source: World Bank (2001)   *The dependency ratio is the ratio of the non-working-age population (under 15 years old and over 64 years old) to the working-age population (ages 16 to 64).

The theory of Malthus

In 1798 the Reverend Thomas Malthus in his *Essay on the Principle of Population* argued that a population trap existed which caused per capita income to remain at low levels. He claimed a universal tendency for the population of a country to grow geometrically (2, 4, 8, 16 etc.) while food supplies could only grow arithmetically (2, 4, 6, 8 etc.). Food supplies could only grow slowly due to the law of diminishing marginal returns. Eventually, shortages of food would check the population growth by causing high death rates. Per capita food output (and hence per capita income, if we assume a purely agrarian economy) would always come back to the same level in the long run. Malthus urged restraint on the part of potential parents as the only solution to the problem.

There is some evidence of population growth in developing countries periodically being checked by food shortages. This must be set against ever growing agricultural productivity in the developed world: technological progress would appear to have invalidated Malthus's theory. The world is now capable of producing more than enough food to meet the basic dietary requirements of its entire population. The problem is essentially one of the distribution of that food. For all this, Malthus's work should not be discarded. While the law of diminishing returns remains a constraint in developing countries, population control can be regarded as important in attaining higher living standards.

Why do birth rates fall as development occurs?

There are a number of possible reasons for this:

- Lower death rates. Families may set a target for the number of surviving children. If death rates are low, this target can be achieved from fewer births.

- Development may reduce the incentive for families to aim for a high number of children. Families in poverty may aim to have many children because child labour can be a valuable source of income and provide the security of having someone to look after you in old age. Having a large family may not be seen as so necessary when this poverty is alleviated.

- At early stages of development the cost of having children is low. This is because they cost little to feed and the opportunity cost of the mother's time spent in child care is small, given the low income available to her if she chose to work instead.

- Knowledge of the economic and social consequences of rapidly growing populations may increase as development occurs.

Policy on population growth

There are a number of policies that governments in developing countries might employ to try to limit population growth, besides the general policy of boosting economic growth.

Educational programmes have an important role to play. The government can supplement these with family planning programmes, offering contraceptives and advice on their use. Most countries now have an official programme of this kind.

Development may reduce the incentive for families to aim for a high number of children.

Circumstances in countries with low levels of development combine to provide an incentive to have high numbers of children. The government is in a position to change these incentives. One example is the reduction of any maternity benefits which are offered. Similarly, fines could be imposed for having high numbers of children. Establishing an old-age security programme would also remove one of the causes of large families. Policies to improve the economic status of women could increase the opportunity cost of having children. Improved education and employment opportunities for women are crucial in this regard.

More draconian measures are sometimes employed, such as China's strict one child rule which forbade couples to have more than one child without express permission, a policy enforced through heavy fines. It was not until late 2013 that a reform was adopted to allow couples to have two children if either parent is an only child.

Were countries to wish to encourage population growth, some of these policies could be reversed. Tax concessions could be offered to provide greater incentives for child birth, for example. Some economists do argue population growth fosters development and should be encouraged. Larger populations generate higher product demands, permitting greater economies of scale. A low cost labour force is also provided, enhancing international competitiveness. Population growth could induce investment by making capital scarce in relation to labour, causing returns to capital to rise.

Conclusion

Population issues are inseparably linked to the study of development. Stabilisation of a country's population has tended to go hand in hand with the achievement of the goals of development. Because development is itself perhaps the primary cause of declining birth rates, it might seem that underdevelopment is the central problem and that tackling it is the key to population control. This, however, would be to neglect the range of potentially effective policies that a developing country can use to lower birth rates. Population control and development should be seen as mutually supporting goals.

The role of migration in causing urban population growth

A feature of the experience of developing nations in recent years has been the rapid growth of urban areas. The populations of many cities have grown at a rate that has made it difficult for them to provide enough jobs, adequate housing and other basic necessities. Concentrations of large numbers of people have also caused great environmental problems.

Rapid urban population growth has two causes. The first is the fast growth of overall population that is associated with the position of developing countries in stage 2 of the demographic transition. This factor affects both rural and urban areas. Rural populations have continued growing in absolute terms because of this, despite the migration of large numbers to towns and cities. This migration is the second cause of urban population growth. Figure 14.1 shows past changes in rural and urban populations and emphasises the rapid growth of urban populations which is expected to continue in developing nations.

Figure 14.1: Urban and rural population change

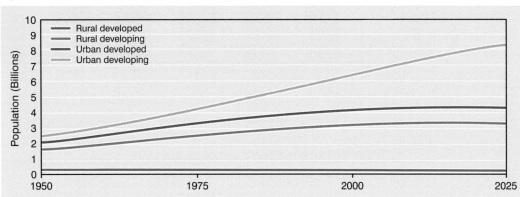

Source: World Resources Institute

Because of the problems associated with over-population of towns and cities, attempts to limit migration have assumed importance in development policy. This is in stark contrast to the view, previously widely held, that migration was essential if development was to occur. The Lewis model of structural change (see Unit 8) argued that migration was necessary for the growth of an urban industrial sector, which would be the engine of economic growth. The urban economy could put to productive use workers who would have had low (or zero) productivity if employed in rural agriculture. Experience increasingly calls this view into question.

Problems associated with rapid urban population growth

Unemployment and *underemployment* have reached disturbingly high levels in many towns and cities. Demand for labour has not risen in line with the rapidly growing labour supply. Because of the inability of urban economies to create jobs sufficiently quickly, many town and city immigrants have been faced by a lower standard of living than they had previously enjoyed in rural areas. Unemployment implies zero productivity for the individuals concerned; even if their productivity had been low in rural areas, this still would have been more economically beneficial. The evidence of substantial urban unemployment undermines the assumptions of the Lewis model.

Much immigrant labour does find employment in the informal economy. This is economic activity that is not registered (see Unit 6). Burdensome regulation in the formal sector increases the costs of registered businesses, making it unlikely that this area can generate the jobs which are needed. Accordingly, the informal sector can be argued to be serving a valuable economic purpose. It does, however, serve to disguise unemployment and underemployment. Those unemployed and seeking work in the informal economy and those working few hours in the same sector are missing from the already disturbing official statistics.

Pressure on the urban housing stock is another problem associated with migration. Many immigrants find accommodation in large slum settlements without access to clean water or sanitation facilities. Figure 14.2 shows that the *number* of people living in slum accommodation in developing countries is still growing, although the rate of growth is slowing down. The *percentage* of the urban population living in slums is falling.

Figure 14.2: Population living in urban slums and proportion of urban population living in slums, developing regions, 1990-2010

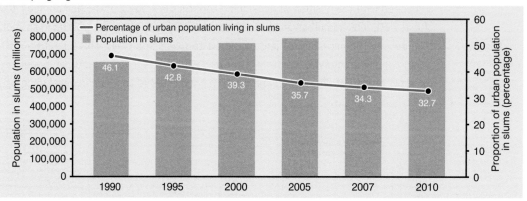

Source: United Nations Millennium Development Goals Report 2010

The over-crowding of cities generates many negative externalities. The spread of disease caused by the unsanitary conditions in slum settlements is one example. Traffic congestion is another, costing both businesses and individuals valuable time. Associated with congestion are high levels of pollution. Air quality in large cities is notoriously poor. This is particularly so in developing countries where cars are likely to be old and inefficient in their use of fuel. Air pollution has serious health implications.

Why does migration continue?

It might seem surprising that migration continues at its present rate, given high levels of urban unemployment. It is usual for economists to assume that individuals are rational in their decision taking and that they will make a choice only if they benefit from doing so. Faced by a high probability of unemployment after moving to a city, it would appear that there is little incentive to make such a move.

One possible explanation is that not all the relevant information is available when migration decisions are made. Rural dwellers might well not be aware of the level of unemployment rates in cities. Even if they are, migration might still make economic sense. This is explained by the Todaro model of migration. In this model, individuals take into account both the probability of finding employment and the likely wage if work is found. Individuals might be willing to migrate if potential wage rates are sufficiently high, even if the risk of unemployment is high too. In essence, this is because the possible gain makes the risk worth taking. The model helps us to understand continued migration within a standard economic framework, but it has been argued that individuals in developing countries are likely to be reluctant to take risks (risk-averse). Urban unemployment is associated with very low, possibly life threatening standards of living. Given that this is so, it is questionable whether potential migrants would find the risk worthwhile.

Policy with respect to migration

The problems caused by migration have in many cases been exacerbated by past government policy. One example is the growth of large slum settlements. Building regulations often mean that much of a city's

Favelas in Rio de Janeiro. Residents have little incentive to improve a house that is not legal.

housing stock is illegal; meeting the required standard entails expense beyond the means of most urban settlers. Forcing settlement in illegal dwellings makes it unlikely that the quality of the housing stock will be improved. Residents have little incentive to improve a house that is not legal. Relaxing regulations so that more housing is legal would also allow legal confirmation of ownership of the houses concerned. Legal owners of property have a valuable, tradable asset which they are more likely to be willing to invest in.

Migration has inadvertently been encouraged by some policies designed to reduce urban unemployment. In line with the Todaro model, policies which increase the chances of finding a job in urban areas raise the incentive to migrate to towns and cities. The net effect on urban unemployment then depends on whether the policy generates more jobs than the numbers added to the labour supply through migration induced by the policy. The negative externalities associated with such migration must also be taken into account in evaluating the policy.

Policy to discourage rural to urban migration is increasingly an important element of government strategy in developing countries. As with attempts to influence any choice, policy must aim to change the relative attractiveness of the various options. In other words, the pattern of incentives must be altered. In particular, the balance between opportunities in rural and urban areas must be addressed. Policies to diversify the rural economy are important. If rural areas are able to offer more employment opportunities, of a greater variety and carrying higher incomes rural dwelling will become much more attractive. This is not to say that development of urban economies to foster higher living standards there should be neglected. Because migration decisions are based upon the relative attractiveness of living in rural and urban areas, the key is to make sure that policy is not biased towards urban development. If it is, the incentive to migrate will remain strong. Should the government place stemming migration high on the list of its priorities, then a bias towards rural development is more sensible.

Educational policy also has an important influence on migration. Evidence suggests that many of those who migrate from rural to urban areas are relatively well educated. This is to be expected because better educated individuals have a better chance of securing well paid employment after moving to the city. Indeed, there is substantial indication that 'qualification inflation' is occurring in many cities. Because of the number of educated workers available, qualifications are being used as a selection criterion for jobs which unqualified workers could do equally well. This means that the valuable human capital embodied in educated workers is not being put to productive use. An implication of this is that governments must address the distribution of spending on education; for example, over-investment in secondary education is likely to be unproductive because of qualification inflation. The resources invested could be put to more valuable use elsewhere. One possible use is to broaden primary education, the goal being universal access. Removing educational inequalities is important in the context of the wider goals of development, because unequal access to education causes inequality of income distribution. Statistics also indicate a very strong correlation between levels of access to primary education and levels of per capita output. Expansion of primary education should encompass both urban and rural areas. Primary education is less specifically geared to the demands of an urban industrial economy than secondary and tertiary education, so it is not likely that this policy will generate an incentive to migrate. Indeed, equal access to education in all areas removes the possible incentive to migrate in search of better educational opportunities for future generations. Despite this, expansion of primary education must be complemented by policies to enhance employment opportunities in rural areas, so that investment in rural education can realise the highest possible return and the incentive to migrate is further reduced.

International migration

It is not only internal migration that is a problem for developing countries. The loss of highly skilled workers through international migration, known as the *'brain drain'*, is also common. Well qualified professionals are often tempted by the opportunity of higher living standards elsewhere. Doctors, scientists and academics are examples of groups where the brain drain is a particular problem. Clearly, developing countries can ill-afford to lose workers possessing such high levels of human capital. The benefits of the investment in the education of workers who migrate in this way are reaped by the developed countries to which they move.

Many developed countries are now seeking deliberately to attract immigrants in order to fill skills gaps and boost the production possibilities of their own economies. This policy could be questioned on ethical grounds, given the likely detrimental impact on developing countries.

It is sometimes argued that even those talented individuals who remain in poor countries pay little attention to the problems of development, choosing instead to specialise in the same sort of areas as their developed nation counterparts. For example, many doctors in developing countries specialise in the study of heart disease. One positive aspect of the 'brain drain' is that 'worker remittances', money sent home by workers who have migrated, are an increasingly valuable source of income to developing countries.

Sustainable development

It is now widely accepted that a vicious cycle exists between poverty and environmental destruction. Much environmental damage is directly attributable to attempts to ensure survival and enhance living standards in the face of absolute poverty; very often the damage done to the environment is permanent and irreversible, depriving future generations of valuable resources. This does not mean that damage to the environment can be avoided simply by removing absolute poverty. The high consumption demands of those who enjoy very high incomes also cause environmental damage: most environmental damage is caused by the billion poorest and the billion richest people on earth.

Because of the problem of permanent environmental destruction, economists have developed the concept of *sustainable development*. One definition of sustainable development is 'meeting the needs of the present generation without compromising the needs of future generations'. Much of the damage presently being inflicted on the environment will limit the productive potential of future generations, as well as lowering living standards in non-material ways. Global warming, for example, makes the world's climate more extreme and less hospitable for human habitation. Deforestation leads to the loss of trees from which people derive aesthetic value, in addition to them being a valuable economic resource. The current economic situation is thus not sustainable in the long term and is still less so given current trends such as the rapidly growing world population. This unit examines a number of specific environmental problems and their causes. Policy options are then considered in the light of the concept of sustainable development.

Environmental problems

A number of specific environmental problems are faced internally by developing countries. Global issues such as climate change must also be considered.

Air pollution. This is a big problem in highly populated urban areas in developing countries, just as it is in developed countries. The problem is moderated to some extent in developed nations by the use of 'clean technologies', although there is much further progress to be made in this regard. Consideration has often been given to the environment in the choice of production techniques, with some plants fitted with modern pollution abatement equipment. Newer cars are fitted with devices such as catalytic converters. Understandably, given low output levels, developing countries are a long way behind in both these regards. Further, government controls on pollution are usually not as stringent. Air pollution in the home is also a big problem in developing countries, largely due to the materials used to provide domestic fuel. These include wood, straw and manure. Struggling for survival, the majority of the population have little choice but to use such fuels for cooking and heat. The damaging fumes emitted, added to other sources of air pollution, are a major cause of respiratory illness. The human cost of suffering is high, particularly when its contribution to premature deaths is taken into account. Treatment costs should also be considered.

Solid and hazardous wastes. The unsanitary conditions created by difficulties in waste disposal were briefly considered in Unit 15. The vast majority of the urban population in developing countries live in slum accommodation, without access to waste disposal services. This is largely because the illegal status of most of the housing prevents it from qualifying for such services. Running sewage in the streets is not uncommon. The health implications are clearly enormous. Problems are accentuated by the blocking of drains and possible pollution of the local water supply.

Water pollution and scarcity. Access to clean water is the exception rather than the rule in most developing countries. Again, this problem has close links to the illegal status of much of the housing. Slum dwellers must buy water at high cost, which even then is rarely fit for human consumption. Valuable resources must be spent on boiling it before it can be used, further contributing to air pollution in the home. Both water scarcity and water pollution are major causes of disease. They can also have damaging effects on the productivity of local businesses.

Soil degradation. The over farming of agricultural land reduces its productivity in future. To remain productive, land needs periods of rest when it is allowed to lie fallow. This is rarely possible while the survival of the farmer and his family is at stake, thus the fertility of the soil declines year on year. The consequence is that long term survival is threatened by the more pressing need to guarantee short term survival. Shortage of land often forces the cultivation of poorer quality land. The fertility of this land also declines rapidly. Soil degradation is a particularly pressing problem where land is held in common ownership and freely available to all. In this situation, much of the cost of over use of land will fall on others. Consideration of the future productivity of land is therefore far less likely to take place when decisions about current use are made.

Deforestation. The loss of tropical rain forests contributes to global warming, because trees are important for absorbing carbon dioxide. Much media attention is focused on the issue in developed countries for this reason. As with many other environmental difficulties, the root cause of this problem lies in poverty. The desperate need for wood to use as a domestic fuel is one of the reasons why forests are cleared, although sometimes the timber is sold abroad to earn valuable foreign currencies. Forests are also cleared in order to provide farming land, despite the fact that the land is frequently marginal for agricultural purposes. Deforestation contributes to soil degradation in another way too. A valuable wind break is removed and erosion of top soil occurs. The extent of the problem especially in Africa and South America is apparent from the data in Figure 15.1.

Figure 15.1: Trends in forest cover

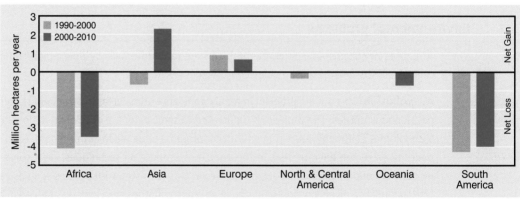

Source: UN FAO

Loss of biodiversity. Deforestation is one cause of the marked reduction in biodiversity in recent years. Many species of animals and plants have become, and are becoming, extinct. Some of these plants and animals have high human use value and might have been used, for example, in developing new drugs. Biodiversity is also valued for its own sake and the morality of human actions leading to extinction is questioned.

Atmospheric changes. Climate change (or 'global warming') is caused by the release of carbon dioxide into the atmosphere. The release of other 'greenhouse gases' such as methane from farming activities also contributes to climate change. Greenhouse gases react with water vapour and ozone in the atmosphere to form a screen that traps solar heat, causing the planet to warm up. Deforestation means that less carbon dioxide is absorbed by trees rather than making its way into the atmosphere. Production and consumption in both developed and developing nations gives rise to the burning of fossil fuels and consequent release of carbon dioxide. The implications of the resulting climate change include more frequent and more fierce storms and floods. Rising temperatures cause ice caps to melt and sea levels to rise, threatening coastal settlements.

A separate problem is damage to the ozone layer through the release of CFCs (Chloro Fluoro Carbons), for example from old fridge cooler circuits and aerosol can propellants. Ozone layer depletion allows ultra violet rays from the sun to penetrate more easily. The effects of this include an increased likelihood of skin cancer.

Environmental damage as an externality

Many environmental problems can be viewed as externalities; that is to say the costs of the environmental damage are borne by third parties, not by the individual agent who undertakes the action causing the damage. No compensation is paid by the agent causing the damage to those who suffer the environmental cost. Consider the example of land that is held for common use. Individuals do not have to pay to use the land and will therefore choose to use it as long as they gain any benefit from doing so. They neglect the resulting decrease in productivity for other users of the land, both present and future. Pollution and global warming arise from economic agents treating the environment as a resource in common ownership: in the absence of government regulation no charge is made for polluting and the environment is freely available for everyone to pump their waste materials into. It is free for firms to emit carbon dioxide, but expensive to install pollution abatement equipment; it is free to allow cars to pump exhaust fumes into the environment, but expensive to fit a catalytic converter; it is free to dump household waste in the street, but expensive to arrange other means for its disposal. Again, we cannot expect individuals to take environmental damage into account when making such decisions, especially in cases where survival is at stake. In short, an individual can be expected to undertake an action as long as his private benefit from doing so exceeds the private cost that he incurs. The resulting level of pollution cannot be regarded as socially optimal. In other words, it is not the best outcome for society.

Figure 15.2 details some of the likely impacts of climate change, while Figure 15.3 highlights the fact that high-income countries contribute disproportionately to emission levels.

Figure 15.2: Projected impacts of climate change

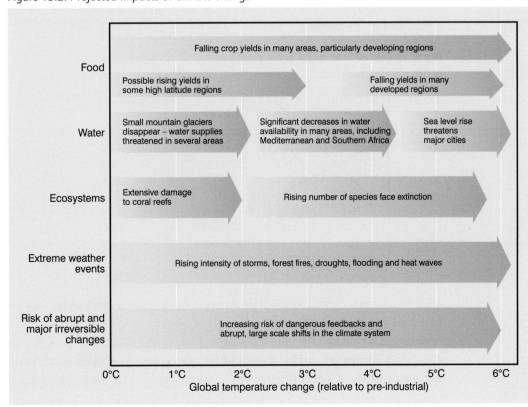

Source: Stern Review on the Economics of Climate Change

Figure 15.3: Share of global emissions, historic and 2005

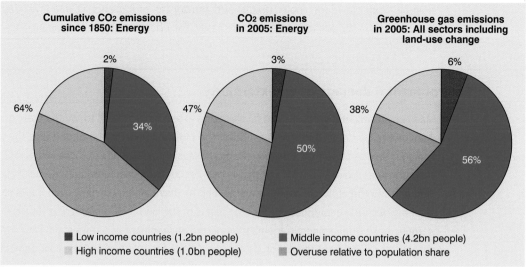

Source: World Bank, World Development Report 2010

Figure 15.4 represents externalities as an example of market failure. A perfectly competitive market brings the demand and supply of a product into line with one another. The supply of the product is based upon the marginal (private) costs of production (MPC). The last consumer on the demand curve receives no consumer surplus, paying exactly the highest price he is willing to pay for the good. The price paid is therefore a measure of the satisfaction received from the last unit of the good consumed, and the demand curve links the quantity demanded not just to price, but also to marginal (private) benefit (MPB). The equilibrium position (P;Q) therefore equates marginal private cost and marginal private benefit, as well as supply and demand. As long as there are no externalities present, a socially optimal level of output is achieved: expanding output any further would impose a higher marginal cost than the marginal benefit derived and would therefore not raise net benefit. Equating marginal private costs and benefits is only optimal as long as these functions represent the marginal costs and benefits to society too, which is true if there are no externalities.

Figure 15.4: Social optimality in the presence
of negative external costs

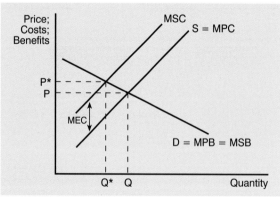

If the production and consumption of the good generates negative externalities, for example pollution, the market no longer produces the best outcome. If a constant marginal external cost (MEC) is generated as more output is produced then the marginal social cost curve (MSC) lies above the marginal private cost curve and is parallel to it. Marginal social cost is now equated to marginal social benefit at a higher price and lower quantity of output (P*;Q*).

The sense in which the marginal social cost equals marginal social benefit condition is socially optimal should be made especially clear, given the development context. If this condition is fulfilled in every market, net social benefit is maximised. This does not mean that the distribution of benefits is to be considered desirable. Indeed, in a market economy the distribution of these benefits tends to be highly unequal which is not likely to be helpful in meeting the objectives of development.

The costs of achieving sustainable development

The external costs of environmental damage are enormous, particularly where permanent and irreversible destruction of the environment occurs. Costs in terms of health and lost production are large. The externality problem is accentuated because the costs are often borne by future generations, meaning that there is still less incentive to take the environment into account when making decisions. There is a clear need to limit the extent of some polluting activities and outlaw others altogether. If a situation persists where economic activity leads to a net loss of resources available to future generations, the situation will not be sustainable.

Some sacrifices are necessary to ensure sustainable development, but there is much controversy about who should make them. In the process of reaching their current living standards, developed countries have been responsible for large scale environmental destruction. Similarly, developing countries feel that they need to use environmental resources to achieve growth and that they are in a position where they can ill-afford to make sacrifices. It is certainly true that developed countries can do much to limit emissions of harmful greenhouse gases, but inevitably much of the focus will fall on the developing world. A key question is therefore how much developed countries should be willing to help developing countries meet the costs of limiting environmental damage.

Policy options

Establishment of property rights

The problems associated with common ownership indicate a need for the establishment of private ownership of land. Other types of land reform are needed as well. Where production is undertaken by tenant farmers, they have little incentive to undertake investments which will enhance the productivity of the land. This is because some or all of the benefit is likely to be appropriated by the landlord. Dividing land into smaller parcels and transferring ownership to the tenants makes it much more likely that the necessary investments will take place. The legalisation of currently illegal urban houses also provides the owners with an incentive to invest in important facilities, such as sanitation.

Government spending

Provision of basic services such as clean water and sanitation can have a remarkable impact in lessening the extent of environmental problems. Because such services improve health and raise productivity they often prove cost effective; large gains can be made for relatively small outlays. Attention must be paid, however, to the distribution of such investment between urban and rural areas. If a bias is shown towards urban areas, this is likely to induce greater migration. In general, careful consideration must be given to the allocation of what funding is available. Evidence suggests that the productivity per pound spent is lower on large projects than on small ones. This implies a need to ensure wide distribution of funding in order to achieve maximum benefit. Very often, government programmes have focused on large scale investment projects. This is a situation that needs to be remedied.

Policies to reduce pollution

- **Regulation.** This simple method involves putting legal restrictions on the amount of pollution that each firm is allowed to generate. Modern economists tend not to favour this method because of drawbacks that include: (i) Informational problems: It is difficult for the government to judge how much pollution to allow; (ii) The regulations apply to all firms, even those that find it very expensive to control pollution, so regulation may be an inefficient method of reducing pollution to the desired level; (iii) Administration (enforcement) costs of the policy may be high. This problem of policing is relevant to any system designed to reduce pollution levels.

- **A pollution tax.** In theoretical terms, the aim here is to charge each firm a tax equal to the externality that it generates. The effect, in terms of Figure 15.4, is to shift the supply curve to the left, so that it is now equal to the MSC curve. The social optimum is thus achieved. The burden of the tax is shared by the consumer and the producer in proportions determined by the relative elasticities of the demand and supply curves.

Pollution tax

Advantages	Disadvantages
The tax meets the 'polluter pays principle'. The producer and consumer are jointly responsible for generating the externality and share the burden of the tax.	Informational problems: It is difficult to judge the level at which the tax should be set.
The tax puts a certain price on each unit of pollution generated. This certainty aids business planning in comparison to any scheme where the price of pollution fluctuates.	Administration/enforcement costs of the scheme may be high.
The tax, if set high enough, will encourage some firms to invest in specialist equipment to reduce pollution emissions.	

- **Tradable pollution permits.** This system is also sometimes known as 'emissions trading' or a 'cap and trade' scheme. The authorities set a cap on the level of pollution emissions by the number of permits they decide to issue to firms. Firms with spare permits are able to sell these permits on to other firms.

Tradable pollution permits

Advantages	Disadvantages
Pollution permits are often judged to be an efficient method of reducing pollution. Those firms that find it cheap to control pollution are likely to do so, and then sell any spare permits to those firms that find it expensive.	Informational problems: It is difficult to judge the level at which the tax should be set.
The externality is internalised (brought within the market system) because the scheme allows the price of polluting to be determined by supply and demand of permits.	Administration/enforcement costs of the scheme may be high.
The initial distribution of permits can be used to address a lack of equity in the distribution of income. In an international emissions trading scheme, for example, developing countries may be allocated more permits per head of their population than a developed country.	The price of polluting may fluctuate according to supply and demand conditions in the permit market. This makes it difficult for firms to plan and may discourage them from investing in equipment to reduce pollution emissions.
	The newly created permits market may itself be subject to market failure

Preventing the spread of disease is the sixth of the Millennium Development Goals (MDGs) (see Unit 1). Particular attention is paid in the MDGs to two important diseases affecting economic development, HIV/AIDS and malaria. The target is to "have halted by 2015, and begun to reverse, the spread of HIV/AIDS and the incidence of malaria and other diseases".

The HIV/AIDS pandemic

HIV (human immunodeficiency virus) is usually sexually transmitted. Those contracting the virus may show no symptoms for a long period of time afterwards. The onset of AIDS (acquired immunodeficiency syndrome), which is the disease resulting from HIV, may take 20 years or longer. However, the average length of time between contracting HIV and developing AIDS is eight to ten years.

It can be seen from Figure 16.1 that by 2011 34 million people were living with HIV globally. However, the number of new infections each year has shown a trend decrease since 1996. This is likely to be due in a large part to increased awareness of the condition and wider knowledge of 'safe sex' practices that can help to protect against infection. Further spread of this knowledge remains important (see the following section).

Figure 16.1: People living with HIV, 2011 (millions)

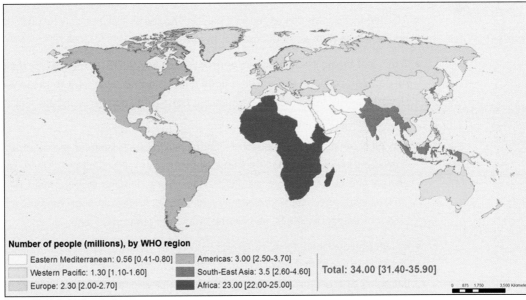

Source: World Health Organisation

Figure 16.2: HIV prevalence in Sub-Saharan Africa continues to fall

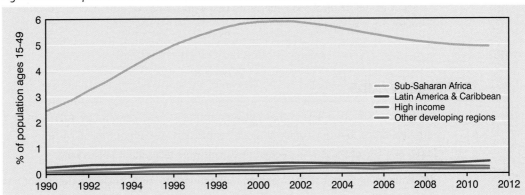

Source: Joint United Nations Programme on HIV/AIDS and World Development Indicators database

Developing regions suffer disproportionately from HIV/AIDS. Over 60% of all cases globally are in Sub-Saharan Africa, although Figure 16.2 shows an improving situation. Women in this region are particularly affected. According to the Report for the Commission for Africa, the reasons include that "Women have a greater biological vulnerability to infection, earlier onset of sexual activity, lower socio-economic status and economic dependence. They are unable to negotiate safe-sex and experience high levels of violence and discrimination." Young people are also disproportionately affected, accounting for around 50% of all new infections.

HIV/AIDS as a constraint upon development

Ways in which HIV/AIDS can reduce economic development include:

- Increased death rates and reduced life expectancy. The suffering as a result is not confined to the person carrying HIV/AIDS. The disease also affects children left behind when their parents die, children born with the virus due to their parents carrying the infection, and grandparents who may be pressed into caring for the children.

- HIV/AIDS imposes health care costs on suffering households. This involves the opportunity cost of sacrificing other areas of expenditure. This may involve not being able to provide other basic necessities such as food or shelter in some cases.

- Affected households may experience reduced income as sufferers may be unable to work or may not be able to work as productively as before.

- Traditional coping mechanisms are undermined by HIV/AIDS (as reported by the Commission for Africa). For example, those with a good harvest would once lend to those with a poor one. However, as HIV/AIDS reduces productivity, those with good harvests have smaller surpluses and are less able to lend in this way.

- HIV/AIDS can put an enormous strain on the health care systems of the countries most affected. This occurs in two ways. Medical staff may themselves fall victim to HIV/AIDS, resulting in fewer doctors and nurses being available. Further, rising demand for treatment for HIV/AIDS can stretch health care systems to breaking point. Again, there is an opportunity cost here. Resources used for treating HIV/AIDS are diverted away from other treatments.

- By reducing the labour force, HIV/AIDS reduces the capacity of the economy and limits economic growth. The loss of highly skilled labour (workers with high levels of human capital) is particularly damaging to economic growth. The UN Human Development Report 2005 states that Zambia now loses two-thirds of its trained teachers to AIDS, and in 2000 two in three agricultural extension workers in the country reported having lost a co-worker in the past year.

The constraints on development discussed above can also be applied to other diseases such as malaria and tuberculosis.

Tackling HIV/AIDS

A relevant distinction here is that between treatment and prevention. AIDS can be treated using anti-retroviral drugs, but this comes at a substantial cost. Despite a tripling of funding in the three years to 2004, only 8% of those who needed treatment were receiving it at this time.

Prevention aims to reduce the numbers contracting HIV/AIDS. There are significant obstacles to achieving this. Lack of knowledge about the disease and the way in which it is transmitted is one of these. There may also be a reluctance to talk about a disease which is transmitted sexually. In some countries, such as Uganda, education has proven highly effective using the clear message ABC – Abstain or delay sex, Be faithful, use a Condom. However, in other areas, cultural barriers may make such a message ineffective, and it would seem that individual cultures need to be taken into account when drafting prevention policies. Overall, it seems clear that there is a need for substantial funding. This includes funding for education, but also for contraceptive supplies and family planning. Spending on contraceptive supplies and family planning is likely, according to research, to prove cost-effective.

Malaria

Figure 16.3: Cause of death among children under five in Africa, 2008

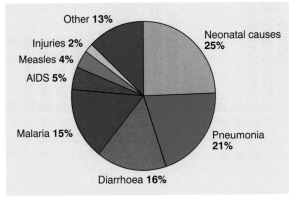

Source: United Nations, Millennium Development Goals Report 2010

Malaria is an infectious tropical disease and causes around a million deaths annually. Again, Sub-Saharan Africa is the worst affected area, accounting for 85% of these deaths. Malaria is spread through the bites of infected mosquitoes and its symptoms include fever, shivering, joint pain, vomiting, anaemia and convulsions.

The constraints imposed on development by malaria are similar to those of HIV/AIDS (see the box earlier in this unit). Figure 16.3 shows that almost one in every six child deaths in Africa is due to Malaria.

Tackling malaria

While malaria is treatable after it has been contracted, the most cost-effective method of tackling the problem is likely to be to prevent it being caught in the first place. A simple mosquito net costing US$2-$5 is effective in preventing malaria for a household. Jeffrey Sachs, Economic Adviser to the United Nations on the Millennium Development Goals, has estimated that malaria can be controlled for $3 billion a year. In terms of a cost-benefit analysis, this appears to represent very good value for money indeed. The World Bank estimate that malaria cost Africa $12 billion annually in lost productivity when it was at its peak.

Although mosquito nets may appear cheap they are likely to appear unaffordable to those living in absolute poverty. It is worth remembering that large numbers of Africans live on less than $1 a day. Economically, the purchase of a mosquito net is an investment, requiring the sacrifice of current consumption. Those living in extreme poverty cannot easily afford to make this sacrifice. This means that the money to tackle malaria needs to come from foreign aid. In 2004, political pressure helped to bring about a pledge of $500 million from the USA to help control malaria.

Mosquito nets will not be affordable to those living in absolute poverty.

This funding saw a five-fold increase in the production of insecticide-treated mosquito nets by 2009 as compared to 2004, helping to reduce the annual number of deaths due to malaria from around 3 million to around 1 million. However, Figure 16.4 shows that the proportion of children sleeping under mosquito nets is still worryingly low in many African countries.

Figure 16.4: Proportion of children under five sleeping under insecticide-treated mosquito nets, 2010-2012 (%)

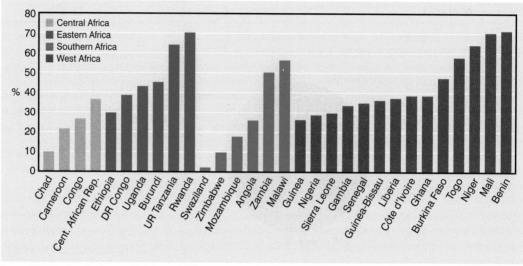

Source: UN Millennium Development Goals Report 2013

Treating HIV/AIDS or preventing malaria?

Preventing malaria through the mass provision of mosquito nets is an example of what might be termed a 'quick win' in terms of health care. It provides impressive results very speedily at a relatively low cost. Other examples of 'quick wins' are given in Figure 16.5.

As great as the suffering and economic loss caused by HIV/AIDS is, many economists suggest that funding should be switched from treating HIV/AIDS to preventing malaria. This is because of the dramatic results achieved at low cost through malaria prevention. Although a harsh judgement to make, choices have to be made where there is limited funding available (the relevant economic concept is opportunity cost) and it would appear that malaria prevention is more cost effective in terms of furthering economic development.

Figure 16.5: Examples of 'quick wins' in the health sector

- The training of large numbers of village workers in health, farming and infrastructure to ensure basic expertise and services in rural communities.

- Distribution of free, long-lasting, insecticide-treated bednets to all children in malaria-endemic zones to cut decisively the burden of malaria.

- Elimination of user fees for basic health services in all developing countries, financed by increased domestic and donor resources for health.

- Expansion of access to sexual and reproductive health, including family planning and contraceptive information and services, by closing existing funding gaps on contraceptive supplies, family planning and logistics.

- Expansion of the use of proven effective combinations for AIDS, tuberculosis and malaria, especially in places where infrastructure already exists but finance is lacking.

Source: The Millennium Project (www.thelancet.com, Vol. 365, 22 January 2005)

International trade and finance

Unit 17: Trade and development

The current international division of labour sees many developing countries specialising in primary produce. Manufacturing is increasingly the realm of newly industrialised countries which have achieved a relatively high level of development. Although developed countries compete in both these areas, they increasingly specialise in the tertiary sector, including financial services.

To a large extent, the position of developing countries as specialists in primary produce is dictated by history (see Unit 4). To understand the discussion about whether this is to their benefit, it is first necessary to study the theory of comparative advantage.

The theory of comparative advantage

Economists from Adam Smith onwards have suggested that specialisation in the production process will realise gains. This is true at the level of the individual firm, with production line techniques where each worker focuses on a particular task. It is true at a national level too, with individual regions specialising in the production of particular goods. Smith's theory is also relevant at the international level. For the sake of simplicity, the example that follows is conducted in terms of just two countries and two products. Suppose that both Neverland and Fantasia can produce both wheat and cloth, and that with one unit of resources the production possibilities are as follows:

	Wheat (units)		Cloth (units)
Neverland	100	or	80
Fantasia	50	or	100

It is clear that Neverland has an absolute advantage in the production of wheat. With the same quantity of resources it can produce 100 units as compared to 50 in Fantasia. By the same reasoning, Fantasia has an absolute advantage in the production of cloth. There will clearly be gains in output if specialisation takes place. For instance, if Neverland removes one resource unit from the production of cloth, using it instead to produce wheat, while Fantasia transfers one resource unit in the opposite direction:

	Wheat (units)	Cloth (units)
Neverland	+100	- 80
Fantasia	- 50	+100
Net gain	+ 50	+ 20

Each resource transfer of this type produces an extra 50 units of wheat and 20 units of cloth, providing the possibility of both countries enjoying higher consumption levels than previously through the process of trade.

The above case is relatively simple because each country has an absolute advantage in one of the two products. The work of David Ricardo, however, suggests that specialisation is still of benefit when this is not so. In our second example, production possibilities with one resource unit are as follows:

	Wheat (units)		Cloth (units)
Neverland	100	or	80
Fantasia	50	or	20

Neverland now has the absolute advantage in the production of both goods. At an intuitive level this might suggest that it has nothing to gain from trading with Fantasia. Note, however, that Neverland has its greatest relative advantage in cloth production. It is four times as efficient at producing cloth but only twice as efficient at producing wheat. Neverland has a *comparative advantage* in producing cloth and should specialise in this area. By implication, Fantasia has a comparative advantage in wheat production. If Neverland transfers one resource unit to cloth production and Fantasia transfers three units into wheat:

	Wheat (units)	**Cloth** (units)
Neverland	-100	+80
Fantasia	+150	-60
Net gain	+ 50	+20

Specialisation and trade can prove beneficial to both nations as long as an appropriate price for exchange can be agreed. The price is known as the *terms of trade* and must lie between the domestic opportunity cost ratios if trade is to be mutually beneficial. In our second example, Neverland can produce one unit of wheat by transferring the resources which could have been used to make 0.8 units of cloth. Because it can obtain a unit of wheat domestically by giving up 0.8 units of cloth, it certainly will not pay more than 0.8 units of cloth to obtain a unit of wheat on the international market. Fantasia has an opportunity cost ratio of one unit of wheat to 0.4 units of cloth. It will therefore want to obtain more than 0.4 units of cloth for each unit of wheat that it sells internationally. One unit of wheat must therefore trade for between 0.4 and 0.8 units of cloth.

The theory of comparative advantage creates a strong argument for specialisation and free international trade. As outlined above, however, it has a number of inadequacies. The model fails to allow for transport costs, for example. These can be substantial when goods are being exchanged internationally, and some trades which would be beneficial without transport costs are ruled out. On the other hand, the theory also ignores the economies of scale that are likely to result from specialisation. These make trade more likely, rather than less.

Economists differ in their opinions about the extent to which specialisation in line with the theory of comparative advantage should take place. There are real dangers to economies in focusing narrowly on a single sector of the economy; if world demand decreases dramatically for the output of that sector then the terms of trade will turn to the country's disadvantage. The same thing could result from a large boost to world supply.

Figure 17.1 shows that agricultural products account for a significant share of the exports of high-income countries, especially the least developed, although this share is in decline. Labour-intensive products account for around 60% of non-oil exports in the least developed and low income countries. This is unsurprising as these nations tend to have plentiful labour forces and are likely to enjoy a comparative advantage in these areas.

Figure 17.1: Low income economies specialise in labour-intensive exports

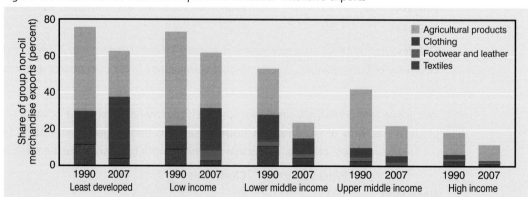

Source: World Bank, World Development Indicators 2010

Declining terms of trade in developing countries

The possibility of declining terms of trade has become a reality for developing nations; the reason for this is encapsulated in the *Prebisch-Singer* hypothesis. This suggests that countries which focus on exports of primary produce will experience continual deterioration of their terms of trade. This is largely because of rapid increase in world supply, due to improvements in technology allowing ever more efficient methods of production. Such methods of production are largely the reserve of developed countries. Because demand for primary produce is price inelastic, prices of primary produce must fall dramatically to mop up the increases in supply. This is compounded by low income elasticity of demand. As world income continues to grow, demand for more income elastic manufactured goods will grow faster than demand for primary produce. Accordingly, the prices of primary produce are likely to decline relative to those of manufactured goods, which developing countries need to import.

The data in Figure 17.2 provides evidence of a long term trend decline in food prices from 1960 to 2004. However, the years since 2004 have seen some marked increases in food prices sparked by factors such as the increase in demand for grain for use in biofuels and growing food demand in emerging markets. This increase in price is helping to support rising income in some developing economies, notably in Africa.

Figure 17.2: World food prices, 1960-2012

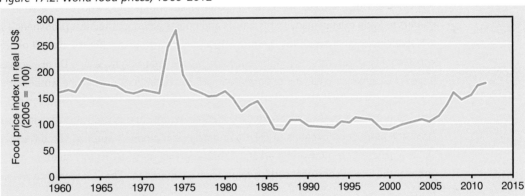

Source: Worldwatch Institute/World Bank

Where does the comparative advantage of developing countries lie?

Common sense suggests that there are some types of primary produce in which developing countries have a comparative advantage. The climate in most of the developed world, for example, does not favour the growing of tropical fruit. Equally, some developing countries are blessed with deposits of oil or minerals. This is very much to their benefit and a valuable source of income.

It is apparent, however, that developing countries are struggling to compete in many international markets for primary produce. This does not itself imply that they do not have a comparative advantage in these areas. Given current conditions, developing countries would have great difficulty in producing most manufactured goods. A unit of primary produce is therefore cheap in terms of the sacrifice of manufactured output; very little, if any, manufactured output would be produced by transferring over the resources which could have been used to gain a unit of primary produce. While acknowledging this, it is not possible for developing countries to satisfy the world's demand for primary produce. Very often, they cannot grow enough basic foodstuffs to feed their own populations. This means that primary produce must be grown in the developed world, where it is likely to be grown at lower absolute cost. If farmers in developed countries grow surpluses to trade, it is clear that the produce of the developing nations may not be competitive.

The necessary implication of the analysis of this and the preceding section is that developing countries need to diversify. The first stage is likely to be to encourage domestic production of simple manufactured goods for domestic consumption. This avoids the need to import goods at unfavourable terms of trade. This is the policy of import substitution, discussed in Unit 9. Because simple manufactured goods favour the use of labour-intensive methods, it is likely that developing countries can then go on to establish a comparative advantage in these areas. Output can be expanded and the surplus exported. The change in the composition of exports should result in improving terms of trade. This is very much the experience of many newly industrialised countries in recent years. It becomes clear that a static analysis of comparative advantage, fixed at a given point in time, is inadequate. There is a need for forward looking strategies, specifically designed to forge new areas of comparative advantage.

Tourism

Tourism is an increasingly important source of foreign exchange earnings for many developing countries. Such diversification of economic structure makes sense on the grounds that tourism is a labour intensive industry, but relatively undemanding in terms of human skills. The world tourist market is also growing in response to increasing world incomes. Tourism has a relatively high *income elasticity of demand*. See Unit 10 for more details on the importance of tourism to developing countries.

Economic analysis of protectionism

The world of free trade envisaged by comparative advantage theory does not exist in reality. Protectionist barriers to trade exist in many forms, tariffs and quotas amongst the most prominent. Figure 17.3 provides a diagrammatic analysis of the welfare impact of a tariff, a specific tax placed on each unit of a good imported. The domestic supply and demand functions are given by S_d and D_d respectively. The initial world price is P_w, at which price any quantity required can be imported from the world market. Q_t is consumed at this price, of which Q_d is supplied by domestic producers. If a tariff is imposed on imported produce such that the price rises to P_{w+t}, then a total of Q_t' is now consumed, reducing consumer surplus as indicated. Domestic production expands to Q_d', raising domestic *producer surplus*. The difference between Q_t' and Q_d' is purchased on the world market, generating revenue equal to this quantity multiplied by the tariff. Some of the loss of consumer surplus remains unaccounted for. This is known as a *deadweight welfare loss*.

Figure 17.3: The welfare effects of the imposition of a tariff

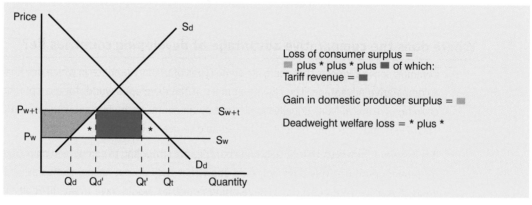

The deadweight welfare loss can be argued to be a reason for countries to remove their own protectionist measures, even if they find that other countries do not reciprocate. This argument may be misleading, however. It presents a static analysis, ignoring the needs of countries to develop their economic structure over time. Thus, it is often accepted as valid for developing countries to use protectionist measures while attempting to nurture the industrial sector of their economies. This is the 'infant industry argument', whereby protectionism is justified by the high average costs faced by emerging industries in relation to their established competitors. Without protection infant industries might die before they get off the ground.

Globalisation

Globalisation describes the process by which the economies of the world are becoming increasingly integrated. In short, they are becoming more like a single economy rather than a series of separate economies.

There are a number of factors driving globalisation. They include:

● Reductions in trade barriers through multi-lateral agreements (facilitated by World Trade Organisation talks).

● Reduced costs of transportation of goods.

● Improved communications (for example, mobile telephones, of which there are greater numbers than landlines in developing countries; also, the internet).

● Reduced barriers to labour mobility, making it easier for workers, especially skilled workers, to choose where in the world they wish to work.

● Increased openness to foreign direct investment by multinational companies.

● Reduction and removal of controls on the movement of financial capital from one country to another.

The net effect of this is that there is more trade in goods and services as time progresses and also greater mobility of factors of production. One consequence is that world trade as a percentage of global GDP increases.

The chart below shows that the growth rate of trade (represented by exports) has been much faster than the growth of global GDP over the past 60 years.

World merchandise exports and GDP, (% changes) 1950-2012

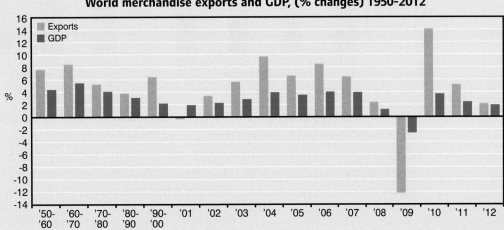

Source: World Trade Organisation, World Trade Statistics 2013

There are many potential benefits of globalisation. These include a stimulus to global output through international specialisation in line with comparative advantage. Access to a global market may generate greater economies of scale, while international competition puts downward pressure on prices, reducing inflation. It is sometimes argued that these benefits are enjoyed primarily by consumers in the developed world, for example when they purchase goods that have been made using cheap labour in developing countries. A major concern associated with globalisation is its contribution to climate change. The transportation of goods by air generates large releases of carbon dioxide into the atmosphere.

(continued overleaf)

The trend towards globalisation has a number of implications for developing countries. These include:

- The choice of inward or outward looking policies (see Unit 9). In practice, the trend towards globalisation may make an outward looking strategy essential. Developing countries may have to reduce their own trade barriers in order to qualify for aid from international institutions or in order to secure reductions in the trade barriers of developed nations in markets such as agriculture and textiles, which are both important sources of foreign exchange for developing countries.

- The need for 'good governance' in order to be in a position to take advantage of the opportunities offered by globalisation.

- The need to be internationally competitive in terms of price and/or in terms of non-price factors such as quality and innovation. The greatest asset of developing countries in trade is possibly its cheap, abundant labour. This advantage may be reduced if the development process generates higher wage levels. At this point it becomes more important to be competitive in non-price terms.

- Cultural implications. It is sometimes observed that as the economies of the world are becoming increasingly homogeneous, so cultures are becoming homogenised, with cultural differences being reduced. Developing countries may struggle to protect their own unique cultures in a globalised world.

It is apparent from the chart below that the share of world exports accounted for by developing countries is increasing over time.

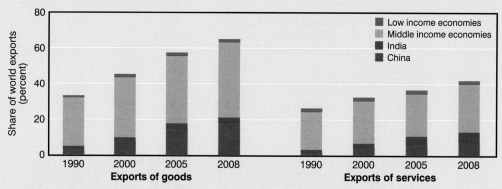

Source: World Bank, World Development Indicators 2010

However, there is ongoing concern that globalisation has not fully extended its reach in the ways that might most benefit developing countries. These include reduction of trade barriers in agricultural and textile markets by developed countries. Remaining barriers in markets for manufactured goods also hinder developing nations attempting to industrialise. However, development issues were chosen as the focus of the Doha round of World Trade Organisation talks. See the following section and Unit 21 for more details.

Protectionism by developed nations

The trade policies of developed countries have received much criticism because of the difficulties they pose for developing countries. Developing nations attempting to industrialise find difficulty in gaining access to markets in the developed world because of protectionist barriers. One reason for such barriers is the structural adjustment necessitated in developed countries by industrialisation in developing nations. Losing manufactured goods markets in which they were once dominant, developed economies have had to restructure in favour of the service sector. Such deindustrialisation carries painful costs. For example, the decline of heavy industry in the UK caused high long term unemployment in the 1980s and 1990s. Economic restructuring requires expensive retraining of the workforce. The pace of deindustrialisation has been slower than it otherwise would have been because of the use of protectionism, enabling domestic

The international debt problem

Many developing countries are burdened by extremely high levels of debt, with the result that funds that could be used to reduce poverty must instead be diverted to making interest payments. This is known as *debt servicing* and does not itself achieve any reduction in the capital sum owed.

The international debt problem is associated with deficits on the current account of the Balance of Payments. When countries fail to earn enough foreign exchange to pay for their imports, the gap is bridged by borrowing.

Debt relief

Relieving developing countries of part of their debt or cancelling it altogether is likely to carry substantial benefits for their development.

The case for such debt cancellation includes the following points:

- Debt cancellation allows developing countries to use funds that would have been spent on debt servicing and capital repayments in ways which will instead foster their own development, such as investment (to encourage economic growth) and measures to alleviate poverty. Campaigners often argue that debt cancellation is a moral duty because of the role it can play in reducing poverty and unnecessary deaths.

- Debt cancellation can be tied to conditions, and these conditions can be drawn up to encourage development. Such conditions might include evidence of low levels of corruption in government, for example. These conditions provide an incentive for more countries to achieve the 'good governance' that helps to stimulate economic growth.

- The breaking of 'cycles of debt'. Many debts are serviced or repaid simply through further borrowing and debt tends to increase over time. This cycle must be broken at some point or development will be very hard to achieve.

- The fostering of development through debt cancellation may be in the long term interests of developed nations. Once development has occurred, for example, bigger markets will exist for the exports of those nations already developed. There is also a link between poverty, disease and, more controversially, terrorism, which can all impact on developed nations.

The policy of debt cancellation is not without its critics, however. Counter-arguments include:

- Debt cancellation may encourage irresponsible borrowing in the belief that the debts incurred may never have to be repaid.

- The cancellation of debt comes at a cost to firms and governments in the developed world to whom the money was owed. For example, the use of public sector money to cancel debt comes at the opportunity cost of diverting money away from public services such as healthcare.

- Poverty exists to a greater or lesser extent in all nations. In developed nations like the UK, absolute poverty is thankfully rare. However, there are still many that are poor in relative terms compared to others in society. Some would argue that governments should tackle poverty in their own countries before diverting resources to tackle poverty elsewhere.

The Heavily Indebted Poor Countries (HIPC) Initiative

In the second half of the 1990s and early years of the new millennium, political pressure for debt cancellation grew. Organisations such as Jubilee 2000 and Make Poverty History lobbied the leaders of the developed world to offer such assistance.

Figure 19.1: The 38 states recognised as the Heavily Indebted Poor Countries (HIPC)

Countries qualifying for full HIPC relief

Countries qualifying for partial HIPC relief

Countries eligible for HIPC relief but not yet meeting necessary conditions

Source: IMF

The Heavily Indebted Poor Countries (HIPC) Initiative was launched in 1996 and provides debt relief with the aim of either cancelling debt or reducing it to sustainable levels. To be considered for the initiative, countries must face an unsustainable debt burden which cannot be managed with traditional means. Figure 19.1 shows the countries considered to be in this position. Assistance is conditional on the national governments of these countries meeting a range of economic management and performance targets. The HIPC initiative has become an important part of the strategy to achieve the Millennium Development Goals (see Unit 1).

Charity concert in Hyde Park in 2007 in support of the 'Make Poverty History' campaign.

Under the terms of the HIPC initiative and a further scheme known as the Multinational Debt Relief initiative (MDRI) the debt stocks of 35 countries have been reduced by over 80 per cent (see Figure 19.2).

Figure 19.2: Reduction in the debt stock of the 35 nations receiving HIPC initiative relief, in US$ billion, end-2009 NPV terms

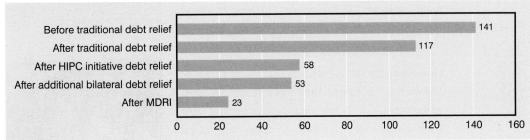

Source: World Bank

Evidence of the effect of the HIPC initiative is offered in Figure 19.3. The HIPC initiative is seen to have reduced debt servicing to around 1% of GDP for those nations receiving relief. This has in turn released funds to be spent on reducing poverty.

Figure 19.3: Average debt service and poverty reducing expenditures in countries receiving HIPC initiative relief

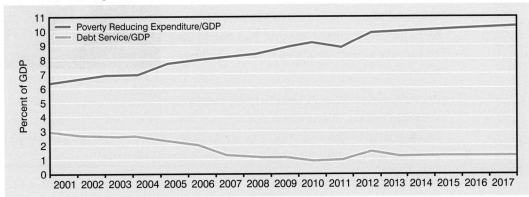

Source: World Bank

Foreign aid

Debt relief or cancellation is one form of foreign aid to help low income countries to meet development objectives. By definition, foreign aid must meet two conditions. Firstly, the donor of the aid must not be motivated by purely commercial considerations. Secondly, concessionary terms are granted on any loan made: the interest rate should be lower and/or the repayment period longer than for commercial loans.

Types of foreign aid

Multilateral aid involves joint assistance from a number of donor countries. The World Bank is an example of a multilateral aid institution.

Bilateral aid involves a donation by a single country to another. A donation or concessionary loan by a national government in the developed world to a government in a developing country would constitute bilateral aid.

Tied aid is given when specific conditions are attached for the offer of assistance. This typically involves the donor country insisting that the recipient nation spend the funds on its exports.

Untied aid allows the recipient country to spend the money received in a manner of its own choosing.

Under what circumstances is aid most beneficial?

All things being equal it would seem desirable that aid should be *targeted* towards those in the greatest need. The push to achieve the Millennium Development Goals has led to a greater focusing of aid on low income countries, although it remains true that much aid still goes to middle income countries.

One reason for this is that organisations are likely to channel aid to where they think it will be most effectively used. Middle income countries are most likely to have the economic structure and sound governmental institutions that are necessary if aid is to be well used.

For developing countries to secure aid, it is becoming increasing important to put into place the conditions that will allow aid to be effectively used. Aid is therefore seen as a catalyst for change in developing nations, as is the case with the HIPC initiative. It is sometimes argued that if aid is well spent it can lead to further development benefits by creating an environment in which the private sector is more likely to invest.

Aid should be targeted towards those in the greatest need.

Generally, untied aid does more to foster development than tied aid. This is because tied aid often serves the interests of the donor country. Although some countries remain highly restrictive, only 12.7% of official development assistance in 2008 was tied. Official aid from many countries, including the UK, is now completely untied.

A number of OECD member countries are now committed to donating 0.7% of their Gross National Income in aid each year by 2013. Their progress towards meeting this target is shown in Figure 19.4.

Figure 19.4: Overseas Development Assistance (ODA) as a percentage of Gross National Income, 2012

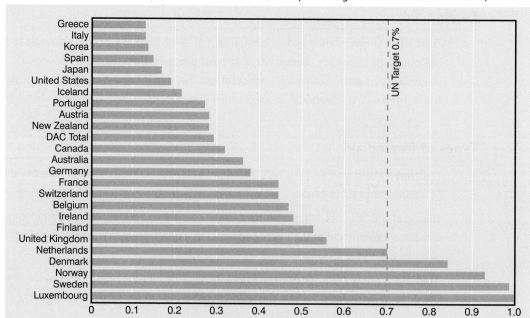

Source: OECD

Level and regional distribution of aid

After a significant fall in aid during the 1990s, total aid levels have risen substantially in the early part of the new millennium and have been maintained at a high level despite the pressures created by the global financial crisis that began in 2007. This is shown in Figure 19.4. The majority of aid goes to countries in Africa and Asia, as can be seen in Figure 19.5.

Figure 19.5: Share of Official Development Assistance (ODA) by region

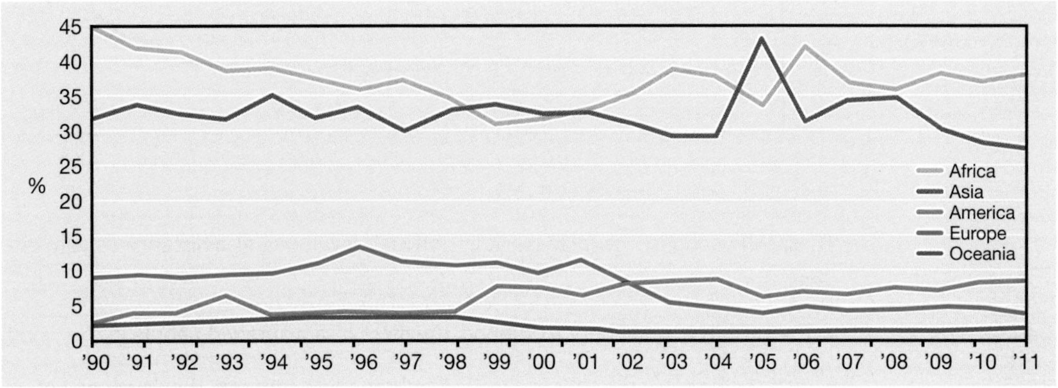

Source: United Nations Development Programme

Aid from non-governmental organisations (NGOs)

Non-governmental organisations are one of the fastest growing sources of aid. NGOs include organisations such as Oxfam, Christian Aid and Save the Children. There is far less cause to question the motivation of unofficial aid than public aid, which often seems to serve the interests of donor nations. Most of the labour force of NGOs work on a voluntary basis, because of commitment to the goals of development. An analysis of the projects funded by NGOs is also revealing. NGOs tend to work on a small scale with local communities on projects which directly widen access to resources needed to meet basic needs, such as water supply, schools and hospitals. The US government has announced its attention to channel half of its aid through NGOs. This reflects a belief in the effectiveness of NGOs in meeting development objectives and a wish to make clear that these objectives are shared by the government. This wish could result from the short term political motive of appealing to the electorate. Alternatively, it might be a recognition that the long term interests of all nations are bound together in an increasingly global economy.

UK Aid (Overseas Development Assistance or 'ODA')

The UK government is committed to providing 0.7% of Gross National Income as aid (known as Overseas Development Assistance or 'ODA'). While other areas of government spending face cuts as part of the austerity programme, aid is increasing so that the 0.7% target can be met. Government spending is set to fall in real terms by 11.5% between the 2010-2011 and 2014-2015 financial years, but aid is expected to rise by 40%.

Politically, the increase in the aid budget at a time of austerity has been highly controversial. Some observers argue that UK government spending should be focused on domestic priorities. There is an opportunity cost to allocating money to aid. For example, the extra money to be given in aid by 2014-15 could have been used to avoid one third of the real terms cut which is to be made to UK spending on education. The path of UK Overseas Development Assistance since 1960 is shown in the graph overleaf.

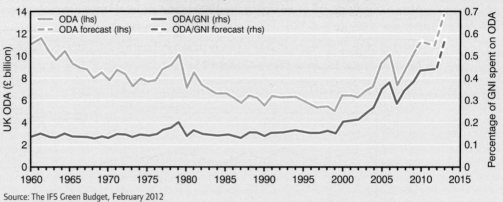

UK Overseas Development Assistance, 1960–2013

Source: The IFS Green Budget, February 2012

Those who support the increase in UK official development assistance usually offer two justifications:

- The UK has a moral duty to support the most disadvantaged people in the world.

- Aid spending is in the UK's interests. If aid spending supports the development of low and middle income economies, then their increasing prosperity may one day make them significant markets for UK exports. There is also evidence that impoverished countries, especially poorly governed ones, may become breeding grounds for terrorism. Some of the perpetrators of acts of terrorism in the UK in recent years are said to have been 'radicalised' during time spent in poorer countries or have perhaps gone to poorer countries to receive training as terrorists.

It is important that aid is spent well to produce good outcomes in terms of development. There is evidence that the quality of UK aid is high by international standards. In a 2010 report on the quality of Overseas Development Assistance produced by the Development Assistance Committee of the OECD, the UK was recognised as an International leader in the field. Some argue that it will be difficult to maintain these standards as the UK tries to meet the target of giving 0.7% of Gross National Income in aid. Standards of aid might drop if too much importance is attached to meeting the target, because not enough attention might be paid to evaluating the development outcomes of the projects financed.

The breakdown of the UK Department for International Development's aid spending by region is shown below:

Breakdown of DfiD aid spending by region, 2010-2011

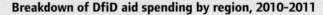

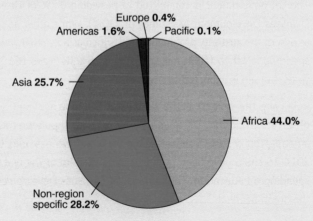

A multinational firm is one which operates in more than one country, by definition having production or service facilities outside the country of its origin. The role of such companies in developing nations is the subject of much discussion. Their presence is welcomed by the governments of many developing countries as a source of investment, given the 'savings gap' which exists between actual savings levels and those required to generate desired levels of investment (see Unit 5). A multinational company is said to undertake *direct investment* in the economy of the recipient country when it purchases productive assets there. This is to be distinguished from *portfolio investment* in developing countries, which entails the purchase of financial assets such as shares, bonds and certificates of deposit.

The operation of multinational companies is a source of employment to the developing world, which should have a multiplier effect on national income. Further, multinationals can help developing nations by introducing new technologies, production techniques and management processes.

In recent years, developing countries have received increasing quantities of direct investment (not withstanding the effect of the global financial and economic crisis that began in 2007), but this has tended to be focused on a handful of rapidly growing economies such as those of China and the BRIC nations (Brazil, Russia, India and China). Figure 20.1 traces FDI inflows to developed and developing economies back to 1995.

Figure 20.1: FDI inflows

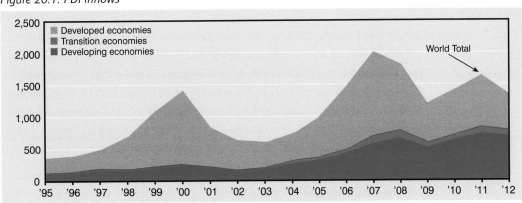

Source: UNCTAD FDI-TNC-GVC Information System, FDI database (www.unctad.org/fdistatistics)

Why do multinational firms locate in developing nations?

A number of factors can help explain the attractiveness of some developing countries to multinational firms. These include:

1. **Protectionist policies adopted by governments in developing nations.** As part of industrialisation strategies (see Unit 9), the governments of developing countries have often used barriers such as tariffs to protect domestic industry. This limits access to the market for firms from other countries. One possibility is to avoid the barrier by producing within the country itself. Because of the employment and tax revenues generated, together with the possibility of domestic industry learning from the techniques of multinationals, governments in developing countries have often welcomed this.

2. **Access to cheap supplies of labour.** The abundant labour supply of developing countries ensures that wages are low. Costs of production are correspondingly lower, particularly in industries which lend themselves to labour-intensive production. As long as cost savings exceed any extra costs generated, the location decision generates a net saving. Such extra costs might include transport costs if the developing nation is more distant from the final market than other countries which could have been chosen for production.

Environmental regulations are often less stringent in the developing world.

3. **Other cost savings.** It is often the case that environmental and safety regulations are less stringent in the developing world than the developed world, or not as rigorously enforced. Not having to comply with demanding regulations can lower costs of production. Further, incentives are sometimes offered by developing country governments. Many provide designated export processing zones (EPZs). These are normally near the coast and benefit from some or all of the following: exemption from import and export taxes; waiving of corporate taxes; availability of premises at below market prices; subsidised utilities including water, gas, electricity and waste disposal; subsidised labour training.

4. **Tax avoidance.** It is possible to use operation in more than one country to avoid taxes. If lower corporate taxes are available in the developing world, location in this area could make sense. Further, it is possible to evade high taxes due on profits made elsewhere. For example, a branch of a multinational firm operating in a developing nation will typically receive many of its resources by a transfer from branches operating elsewhere. To measure the profitability of each branch, a notional sum representing the price of the resource is added to the costs of the recipient branch and to the revenues of the supplying branch. If taxes are lower in the developing world, an artificially low price can be charged on resource transfers. This has the result of the company reporting a higher profit where tax rates are low, and a lower profit elsewhere. Suppose now that tax rates are higher in a developing nation than elsewhere, but location there was still attractive for reasons such as cheap labour. An artificially high resource transfer price could be used, lowering reported profits in the developing nation and thereby avoiding taxation.

Possible development benefits from multinational companies

It is often held that the presence of multinational firms has a beneficial impact in terms of development. This is clearly the view of many governments in developing countries and is encouraged by the IMF. Some of the possible benefits include:

1. **Direct and indirect effects on employment and income.** Multinational companies are major employers in some developing nations, creating much needed income. The impact in terms of jobs and

income is greater when indirect effects are taken into account. Incomes received by employees of multinational firms will be spent, generating employment and income in other areas of the country. There will also be an indirect effect from any backward or forward linkages that the company creates in developing countries. Suppliers of materials to the firm, for example, will enjoy a large boost to demand. In short, the investment undertaken by the multinational company represents an injection into the circular flow of income of the local economy and generates a multiplier effect.

2. **A valuable source of foreign currency.** Direct inward investment represents an inflow on the capital account of the recipient nation's balance of payments. It should, be noted, however, that many other effects on the balance of payments accounts will also result from the initial investment. Any imports of raw materials will represent an outflow on the current account, as will any repatriation of profits. If any of the output produced is for sale elsewhere, this is an export and generates a current account inflow. If output is sold in the country in which it is produced, it is possible that it will replace imports. This reduces current account outflows. It is not possible to generalise as to whether a multinational firm causes a net inflow or outflow of currency over time.

3. **Transfer of expertise and technology to developing nations.** Governments pursuing an industrialisation strategy often welcome the involvement of multinational companies because local firms and entrepreneurs acquire new skills through interaction with multinationals. Exposure to western production techniques and management processes is thought to be a valuable aid to industrialisation. Further, multinational firms use the most modern of machinery and equipment, resources which otherwise would not be available for use in developing nations.

4. **The generation of tax revenues.** Corporate tax paid by multinational companies can be used for a variety of public expenditure projects.

Possible draw-backs of multinational company presence in the developing world:

1. **Widening of income distribution.** Numerous studies have indicated that greater inequality of income results from the presence of multinational companies. This is because of a tendency towards monopoly in industries with a multinational presence. Monopoly power results in high profits (the reward to entrepreneurship) relative to payments to other factors of production. Those who share in these profits then gain relative to others.

2. **Exploitation of local workforce and the environment.** Possible attractions of developing nations to multinational firms include minimal labour regulations (including safety rules) and environmental legislation, these helping to lower costs of production. It can be argued that exploitation of such conditions is not wise for the company, given heightened awareness of such issues in the developed world. Poor publicity would be seriously damaging to the firm.

3. **Possible currency outflows.** As explained in the second point of the previous section, it is unclear whether multinational companies typically generate net inflows or outflows of currency for the local economy.

4. **Contribution to the brain drain.** International migration of highly skilled, productive workers is a big problem for developing countries. It was suggested in Unit 15 that such workers often serve the interests of the developed world even if they do not physically migrate. The presence of multinationals is one possible cause of this. Talented individuals might be employed by multinationals rather than employing their skills in ways that clearly help to meet development objectives.

5. **Stifling of local entrepreneurship.** This is in direct contrast to the claim that entrepreneurial skills are encouraged by interaction with multinational companies. Because multinationals tend to dominate the market for their products in the local economy, barriers to entry to local entrepreneurs are likely to be high. Potential entrepreneurs will be unwilling to take the risk of competing against the might of a large multinational corporation.

6. **Low taxation revenues.** It is sometimes suggested that taxation revenues from multinational companies are not as large as they should be. Low rates are sometimes offered as a deliberate policy to attract direct investment. If higher rates are charged, tax avoidance often occurs through practices such as the use of artificial resource transfer prices (see the fourth point of the first section of this unit).

7. **Use of inappropriate capital intensive techniques of production.** Abundant labour supply in developing countries appears to demand the use of labour-intensive production techniques. Frequently, however, multinational companies use capital-intensive techniques, generating only minimal employment in the local economy.

There are numerous international economic institutions which play a role in development. These include the World Trade Organisation, the International Monetary Fund and the World Bank.

These institutions increasingly cooperate with one another, to the extent that reference is now sometimes made to the 'international development community'. This community extends to encompass institutions which are not wholly economic in nature, such as the United Nations. Within this community, institutions see themselves as playing distinct roles in making progress towards the Millennium Development Goals (see Unit 1).

Trade liberalisation and the 'Washington Consensus'

Any discussion of the role of these institutions in development must recognise that all of them are fundamentally in favour of free trade and that their policies are therefore aimed at reducing barriers to the movement of goods and factors of production between countries. In other words, the institutions promote *globalisation* (see Unit 16) as a means of achieving development. This position has come to be known as the 'Washington Consensus' in virtue of the location of the many development institutions, although the term is often used in a somewhat derogatory fashion.

The international institutions argue that reducing barriers to trade will lead to higher living standards both in developing and developed countries. Estimates by the World Bank suggest that welfare gains from removing barriers to merchandise trade would amount to between $250 billion and $620 billion a year, with up to half of these gains being captured by developing countries.

Not everyone agrees with this view. Some argue that free trade allows powerful developed countries to exploit developing nations, for example by using them as a source of cheap labour. Others argue that rapid globalisation leads to the use of capital-intensive, technologically advanced production methods in developing countries. This might be inappropriate at their current stage of development. Environmentalists cite the negative externalities associated with transporting goods around the globe.

The World Trade Organisation

The World Trade Organisation (WTO) exists to promote free trade. It aims to reach agreements between its members to reduce trade barriers such as tariffs, quotas or overly demanding safety or technical standards which are sometimes used deliberately by governments to deny access to foreign producers to their country's market.

Agreements to reduce trade barriers are often difficult to accomplish. This is because even those governments fundamentally in favour of free trade sometimes have economic or political reasons for wishing to protect particular sectors of their economy from competition. For example, agriculture remains the most protected sector of the global economy, despite its importance to developing countries.

Given such difficulties, 'rounds' of talks designed to reduce trade barriers tend to be rather lengthy. The WTO itself was formed as the successor to the General Agreement on Tariffs and Trade (GATT) as a result of the Uruguay Round of talks. These lasted from 1986 to 1994, while the current Doha round of talks began in 2001!

Figure 21.1 charts the growth of world trade since 1980 and links it to the reduction of tariffs which has taken place over the period, largely as a result of the activities of the WTO.

Figure 21.1: Tariff reductions and increases in world trade

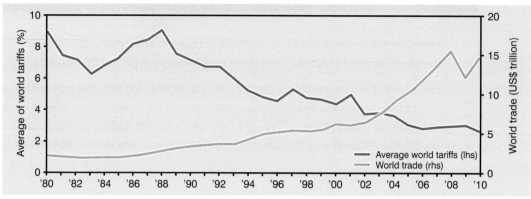

Source: World Bank, World Trade from World Trade Organization report, 2012

Developing nations have often tended to be on the fringes of the GATT/WTO, not signing up to all of the agreements which developed nations have made with each other. This changed at the Uruguay Round, with the introduction of a 'single undertaking' principle. Developed and developing nations now sign up to the same agreements.

The Doha Development Agenda

The Ministerial Conference at Doha in November 2001 put into place the Doha Development Agenda. A key part of this programme was the launch of a new round of trade talks, focused on the needs of developing countries. This was a major step. Whereas the WTO has been perceived at times in the past to serve mainly the interests of rich developed countries, for the first time development has been placed at the heart of its work.

Amongst the topics of the talks are:

1. Reduction of tariffs in agriculture, with a view to increasing the access of developing countries to markets in the developed world. It is also hoped that a substantial reduction in agricultural price support, such as offered by the EU's Common Agricultural Policy, will be achieved.

2. Reduction of *tariffs* on industrial goods, especially on products of special export interest to developing countries, such as textiles and clothing. It had already been agreed in the Uruguay round that quotas were to be phased out in textiles and clothing by 2005.

3. Improvement of the dispute settlement mechanism, with a view to improving the implementation of rulings and participation of developing countries.

Significant progress has already been made in opening up markets to the exports of developing countries. This is demonstrated by the fall in average world tariffs shown in Figure 21.1.

Also part of the Doha Development Agenda is an agreement to ensure that patent protection does not block developing countries' access to affordable medicines. Patents grant monopoly power over the production of new medicines for a number of years to the companies which initially develop them. This monopoly power raises prices, making the medicines unaffordable to developing countries.

The reason for the existence of patents is to provide an incentive to develop new medicines. Monopoly power over the supply of new medicines justifies the investment in the research which is necessary to develop them. A potential problem with the Doha agreement, therefore, is that it reduces the incentive to develop new medicines. Further, relaxing restrictions on patents in developing countries is only effective if those countries have firms capable of producing the medicines. Often, this is not the case.

The Doha round of talks have proven very difficult to bring to a successful conclusion. They were originally scheduled to finish no later than 1st January 2005, but ministerial discussions at Geneva collapsed in July 2008 with no end to the Doha round in sight. Pascal Lamy said: "Members simply have not been able to bridge their differences" adding that out of a to-do list of 20 topics, the positions of negotiating states had converged on 18. As of late 2013, the future of the Doha Round remains uncertain.

The International Monetary Fund

The International Monetary Fund (IMF) was brought into existence at a conference in Bretton Woods, New Hampshire, in 1944. The organisation was designed to bring stability to the global financial system in the post-war period.

A country appeals to the IMF for help when it is experiencing a shortage of foreign currency reserves, either because of the need to finance a deficit on the current account of the Balance of Payments or to support its exchange rate. Such shortages normally imply that the country has been unable to access funding from other sources, such as foreign direct investment or portfolio investment. Thus, the appeal to the IMF normally occurs against a background of crisis. The IMF lends money in order to prevent the disruption to the international financial system which would result from a country failing to meet its commitments to other nations.

While IMF funding can help avert a short term crisis, the fact that a country finds itself in crisis indicates that it is 'living beyond its means'. It is spending more foreign currency than it can earn and if it continues to do so, the crisis will reoccur. For this reason IMF funding is usually of a conditional nature, intended to bring about structural adjustment in the recipient economy. In desperate financial trouble, countries which appeal for help are not usually in a position to refuse the IMF's conditions.

The IMF and development

A number of developing countries have sought IMF help in the last three decades, as current account deficits associated with the international debt problem have become too large to finance. The conditions which the IMF have attached to its lending mean that it has had a key role to play in development in these countries.

The conditions imposed by the IMF have typically included:

- The reduction of protectionist barriers
- Devaluation of the official exchange rate
- Greater openness to foreign investment
- Tight domestic fiscal and monetary policies

These conditions are designed to promote trade-orientated economic growth in the long term. Possible benefits include:

(i) A reduction in domestic inflation as a result of tightening monetary and fiscal policy. The market economy functions more efficiently with low inflation, and the country's exports will be more competitive on price.

(ii) More foreign investment will increase the economy's capacity, shifting its production possibility frontier outwards.

(iii) Devaluation of the exchange rate makes the country's exports cheaper to people in other countries.

(iv) A reduction in protectionist barriers force a country's domestic industries to become more efficient if they are to compete effectively in international markets.

However, in the short term, the imposition of these conditions delivers a sharp shock to the domestic economy. It is possible to argue that the conditions damage development:

(i) Tightening of policy lowers aggregate demand, leading to higher unemployment. Recession is a distinct possibility. Developing countries can ill-afford the reduction in living standards which this implies, even if it transpires to be only short term.

(ii) Evidence suggests that the adjustments insisted on by the IMF hit poor families hardest. For example, fiscal tightening will curtail government spending on projects to meet basic needs.

(iii) Firms in developing countries are likely to struggle to compete in international markets when protection is withdrawn.

The World Bank

Like the IMF, the World Bank was formed as a result of the Bretton Woods conference in 1944. The initial focus of the bank was to provide funding for reconstruction following the decimation of war, as indicated by its full title, the International Bank for Reconstruction and Development. With the job of reconstructing Europe complete, the World Bank has increasingly turned its attention to development issues.

While the IMF is primarily concerned with the external (international) financial transactions of a country, the World Bank is mainly concerned with providing finance for internal investment projects. Lending by the World Bank usually takes place at market rates of interest, meaning that it does not satisfy the definition of an aid institution (see Unit 19). However, in 1960 a branch of the World Bank known as the International Development Association (IDA) was formed. The IDA only lends to very poor countries whose per capita incomes fall below a certain level, and does lend on concessionary terms. Loans made by the IDA are usually interest free and allow long repayment periods.

Early efforts of the World Bank to finance large scale infrastructure investments in transport and communications and utilities like water and electricity delivered relatively small benefits in terms of increased GDP, perhaps because the economies of developing countries were not structured to take advantage of them. From the 1970s, the World Bank has focused on smaller scale projects aiming to meet basic needs, with the 1990s bringing an added emphasis on sustainable development. This means that projects are unlikely to be funded if they cause environmental damage.

The World Bank supports trade liberalisation, which has been a theme of this unit. For example, many of the projects which it finances are designed to help developing countries make the most of the trading opportunities open to them. It also offers advice and technical assistance with a view to encouraging trade.

'Ownership' of policy

Free markets and international trade are playing an increasingly important role in the economic development of poorer countries. This is with the encouragement, or, in some cases, the insistence of the institutions discussed in this unit. There are costs associated with such changes. These include the necessary structural adjustment in developing countries, and the inevitable unemployment which will occur in sectors of the economy which decline as new ones grow. Some would argue against trade liberalisation on the grounds that its success relies on entrepreneurial values which are largely absent in the developing world and requires changes to lifestyles which the populations of developing countries are reluctant to accept.

These concerns are accepted by the WTO, the IMF and the World Bank. However, rather than seeing them as a reason for abandoning trade liberalisation, they believe that efforts must be made to encourage the acceptance of free trade in developing countries. This concept is termed 'ownership'. If free trade is seen as being imposed from outside, and thus meets with resistance, it is likely to fail. On the other hand, success is more likely if trade liberalisation is accepted as necessary or desirable. Success is most likely if the policy is 'owned' by developing countries in the sense that is introduced by them (with outside support as necessary), for their benefit.

Different development amongst developed nations (with specific reference to the EU and the UK)

Introduction

The need for development applies even in nations that are classified as developed. The most developed nation in the world in 2012 was Norway according to the Human Development Index of the UN. Norway achieved an index value of 0.955, leaving substantial room for improvement. In fact, we can probably not make sense of the notion of a country being *fully* developed. This is because we do not know what the limits to possible achievement with regard to per capita income, life expectancy and other development indicators might be. In other words there is always further development to aim for.

There are big differences in the levels of development between those nations that are considered to be developed. For example, the UK human development index value in 2012 was 0.875. This left it lagging some way behind Norway.

It is natural, of course, that development economists should focus on those areas where levels of development are much lower. Here the prevalence of absolute poverty and human misery cries out for attention. However, this is not to say that further development in countries that have achieved high levels of development should be neglected.

Poverty in developed nations

It should also be noted that pockets of poverty exist even in developed nations and that the living standards of different regions within a developed nation can vary widely. Approximately one child in every six in rich developed nations lives in relative poverty.

Figure A1: Relative child poverty rates

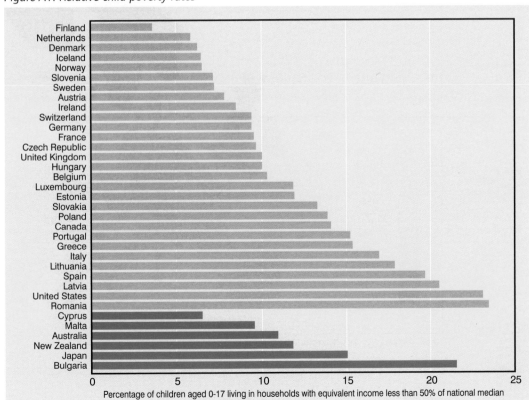

Source: UNICEF report card 11 (2013)   Countries shown in green bars have data for fewer than 75% of all the indicators used

Figure A1 reveals that the performance of the UK is not good with regard to child poverty. It is likely th poverty amongst children (and adults) in the UK is concentrated in certain areas of the country. Levels development differ within countries as well as between countries. This is confirmed by the fact that four regions of the UK were lagging far enough behind to qualify for the most generous type of regional funding from the EU between 2007 and 2013.

Differential levels of development within the European Union (EU) and policies to tackle this problem

Large differences in living standards exist between different regions of the EU and these have grown as the EU has expanded to include Eastern European nations. Luxembourg, the wealthiest member state, has a GDP per capita more than two-and-a-half times the average of the 27 EU member states. At the other end of the scale, Bulgaria and Romania are more than 50% below the average. GDP per capita for the EU as a whole was €25,500 in 2012.

Reducing developmental disparities is a fundamental objective of the European Union and between 2007 and 2013 over one-third of its budget was set aside for regional policy aimed at reducing these differences. In total, €347.4 billion was due to be spent over this period. It was estimated to be possible to boost growth in new member states by as much as 6% and to create two million new jobs.

Figure A2: GDP per capita, price level adjusted, Index, preliminary estimates 2012, EU27 = 100

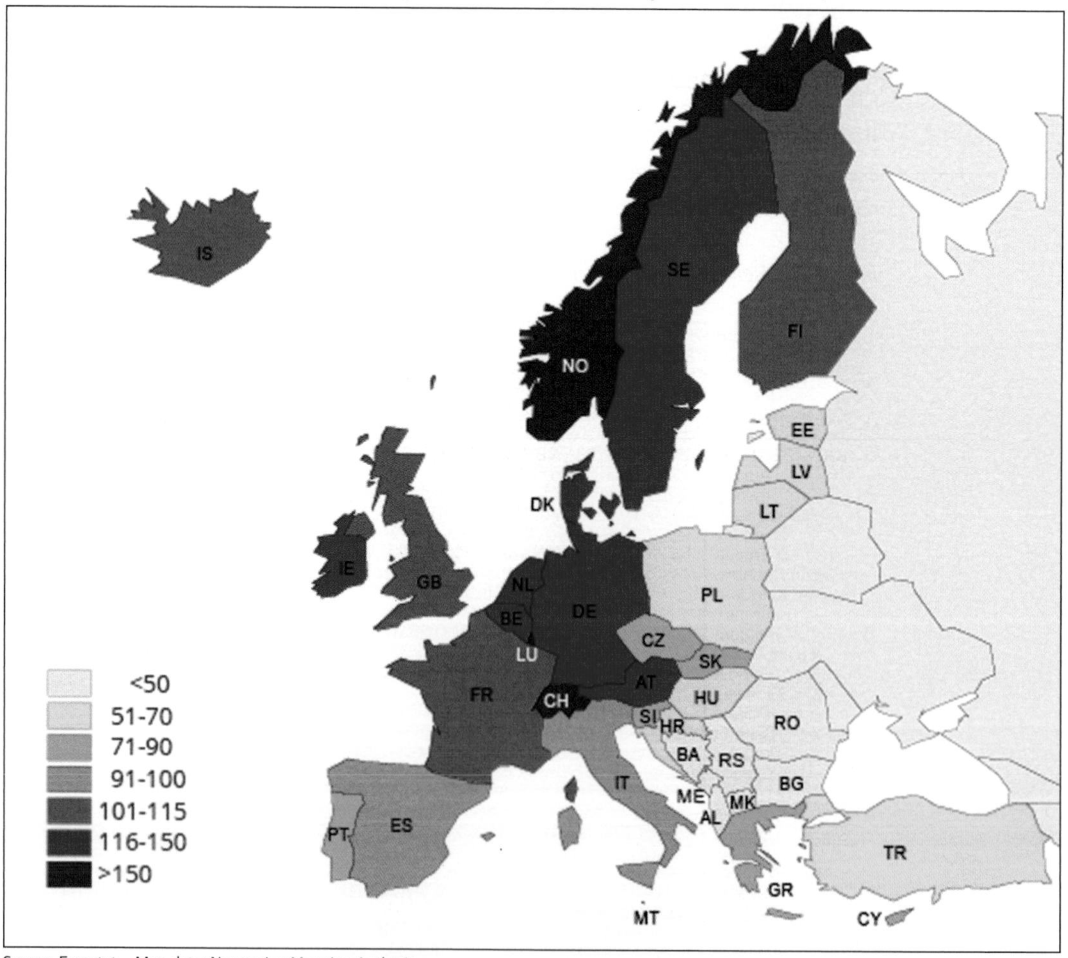

	<50
	51-70
	71-90
	91-100
	101-115
	116-150
	>150

Source: Eurostat   Map data; Norwegian Mapping Authority

...ectiveness of EU regional funding

EU regional funding can provide between 50 and 85% of the total funding for any project. *Additional funding* must be provided by national governments or through new injections of private sector investment. However, it is no longer the case that EU funding has to be *matched* 'Euro-for-Euro' by national governments or the private sector, as was the case from 2000 to 2006.

Member states of the EU must prepare national and regional operational programmes, aimed at ensuring effective planning in order to gain the maximum developmental gain from the spending.

Examples of projects which may be financed through such funding include:

- getting sites ready for industrial development;
- building and refurbishing factories and offices;
- improving transport access to industrial, commercial and tourist developments;
- training and developing local people to equip them with the skills and capabilities to find new jobs, especially in the new industries;
- supporting innovation and development;
- promoting the cultural arts and leisure industries;
- support measures for small and medium-sized companies;
- cleaning up the environment;
- helping those in the most disadvantaged communities.

The effectiveness of EU regional funding

The theoretical argument in favour of EU structural funding may be expressed in terms of the following:

1. The requirement for additional funding ensures a major injection into the circular flow of income of the local economies which qualify for assistance.

2. Regional funding may have a multiple impact on the local economy, as the money spent in the region provides jobs and income. The income generated may be spent in the region generating further jobs and incomes. Increased levels of output may also give rise to further investment (the *accelerator* principle of investment).

3. The allocation of funds through a carefully coordinated programme with specific development goals ensures that the funding is used as effectively as possible.

For each of these points there are potential difficulties:

1. The additional requirements for matched funding can be very demanding. It can be very difficult indeed to raise the outside money required, and this can result in the cancellation of some major projects.

2. The value of the funding may be limited by major leakages from the circular flow of income. For instance, if contracts for major investment projects are given to firms from outside the region this will lead to a smaller multiplier value in the local economy. This was the experience in South Yorkshire when facilities for the Student Games and Sheffield's tram system were constructed.

3. It can prove very difficult to achieve the desired coordination of the programme and to deliver objectives. Also, there are major bureaucratic costs in administering it.

The evidence suggests that the success of EU regional programmes is mixed. From 2000-2006, 94 of the poorest regions of the EU were granted "Objective one" status. While most of these regions (80 of them) saw their GDP increase relative to the EU average, some did not. Of these regions, South Yorkshire saw the third biggest increase in its GDP. It would be wrong to assume that those areas enjoying gains did so solely because of EU funding, but it is likely that the stimulus it provided to aggregate demand was a significant catalyst for growth. It will soon be possible to evaluate the effectiveness of the 2007-2013 regional programme.

Glossary

Absolute advantage A country is said to have an absolute advantage over another with respect to a good that it can produce at lower absolute cost; that is to say, using fewer resources.

Absolute poverty This is said to exist when the income of an individual or group is only just sufficient to support human life.

Allocative efficiency A situation where an economy's scarce resources are distributed between alternative uses in such a way as to maximise society's collective benefit.

Average product Total output divided by the number of units of a given input. For example, the average product of labour is the total output divided by the number of units of labour used in the production process.

Balance of payments A summary record of all the currency flows between a given country and the rest of the world, over a given time period.

Basic needs The goods and services necessary to support a minimal standard of living (food, clothing, shelter, education etc.).

Biodiversity The extent of variety of living species.

Brain drain The loss of highly productive workers to other countries. In the context of development, this usually entails the migration of educated professionals from developing countries to the developed world.

Capital Output which is used for the production of further output.

Capital account The section of the *balance of payments* account that deals with currency flows resulting from cross-border investments, loans and grants.

Capital accumulation Increasing the capital stock, both physical and human.

Capital-intensive techniques A production process which uses a high proportion of capital in relation to other factor inputs.

Capital-output ratio The number of units of capital required to produce a unit of output over a given period of time. For example, a capital-output ratio of 3 would indicate that three units of capital are needed to produce each unit of output (annually, say).

Cash crops Crops grown entirely for the market.

Central planning State determination of resource allocation.

Ceteris paribus The Latin term for 'other things being equal'.

Command economy An economy where resources are state owned and their use determined by *central planning*.

Comparative advantage A country has a comparative advantage over another with regard to a product which it can produce at lower *opportunity cost*, expressed in terms of alternative goods foregone.

Demographic transition The typical pattern of birth and death rates as a country becomes more developed. This is split into three stages, the first exhibiting both high birth rates and high death rates (and thus a stable population), while the second is characterised by high birth rates and lower death rates (and thus a growing population) and the third by low birth and death rates (and thus again a stable population).

Dependency ratio The ratio of the economically [...] the working population.

Devaluation A sharp reduction of a currency's external [...] within a fixed exchange rate system.

Development The process of improving standards of livi[...] both in material (which tends to be the primary focus o[...] economists) and psychological aspects.

Development banks Financial intermediaries providing funds for development projects.

Development plan A government plan detailing development objectives and how they are to be achieved, usually over specific period; for example, five year development plans are common.

Diminishing marginal returns The declining marginal product of a variable factor of production as successive units of the variable factor are added to a given quantity of fixed factor. Diminishing marginal returns set in eventually as more of the variable factor is added, although the *marginal product* is likely to rise initially due to gains from specialisation.

Disguised unemployment A situation in which a resource is employed full-time, but is engaged in unproductive activities for some of the time.

Division of labour *Specialisation* at the level of the firm (with each worker specialising in a particular task) at a national level (with each region specialising in particular products) or an international level (with each country specialising in particular products).

Dualism A sharp division between sectors of an economy (for example, agricultural and industrial sectors) or between the living standards of different groups of people (both within countries and on an international basis).

Economic growth Increases in an economy's productive potential, caused by increases in the quantity of resources available or improvements in their quality. Statistical evidence of economic growth is provided by a long term upward trend of national income.

Economies of scale Reductions in the average cost of production (total cost/total output) as output is expanded.

Exchange rate The price of one currency expressed in terms of another.

Externality The 'spill-over' effect of the actions of an economic agent on third parties, where no compensation is paid. Both negative and positive externalities are possible. An external cost is imposed when a third party is not compensated for his suffering, while an external benefit is enjoyed when a third party does not have to pay for utility that he derives from the actions of another agent.

Financial intermediary A financial institution that channels funds from savers to borrowers.

First world The developed economies of Western Europe, North America, Australia, New Zealand and Japan.

Foreign aid Cross-border grants or concessional loans.

Foreign direct investment (FDI) Overseas investments in physical capital by multinational corporations.

Gains from trade The increase in output (and hence consumption) facilitated by the process of *specialisation* and trade.